WILLIAMS-SONOMA

POTATO

RECIPES AND TEXT
SELMA BROWN MORROW

GENERAL EDITOR
CHUCK WILLIAMS

PHOTOGRAPHS
MAREN CARUSO

SIMON & SCHUSTER • **SOURCE**

NEW YORK • LONDON • TORONTO • SYDNEY • SINGAPORE

CONTENTS

MAIN COURSES

POTATO SALADS

BREAKFAST POTATOES

INTRODUCTION

The modest potato has long played an essential part in cuisines around the world. Incredibly versatile, potatoes can be cooked by almost any method, and their mild and comforting flavor make them an excellent match for so many different ingredients. Yet time and time again, potatoes have been treated as mere side dishes. They need not be limited in this way. The diverse selection of recipes inside these pages demonstrates that potatoes can play a prominent role as a main course or as an integral element of an unforgettable meal.

Throughout this cookbook, each recipe is accompanied by an informative side note that highlights a particular ingredient or technique. In addition, a chapter of basics provides you with all the information you need to bring potatoes to your table in a variety of ways. So, whether you like potatoes mashed and smothered with butter, deep-fried and crisp, or tossed in a refreshing salad, a wealth of delicious potato recipes awaits.

Chuck Williams

THE CLASSICS

The following dishes are classics for two good reasons: They set a standard that endures, and they are always appropriate no matter what the occasion. A creamy potato gratin, hearty potato-leek soup, or batch of crisp French fries never fails to please. Whether the setting is casual or formal, these all-time favorites will fit in nicely every time you serve them.

ROASTED NEW POTATOES WITH HERBS

BAY LEAVES

The gray-green leaves of the laurel tree, bay leaves are used to flavor a wide variety of dishes. When dried, the leaves have a slightly sweet, citrusy, and nutty flavor. Mediterranean bay leaves, especially those from Turkey, are prized for their subtle taste and aroma. They are oval and 1–2 inches (2.5–5 cm) long. California bay leaves, narrower and 2–3 inches (5–7.5 cm) long, have a more pronounced flavor. Both types are sold dried in jars or packets and can be found in the herb-and-spice section of well-stocked markets.

Preheat the oven to 375°F (190°C). Spray a large baking sheet with nonstick olive-oil cooking spray.

In a mini food processor or blender, combine the shallot, thyme, sage, oregano, garlic, bay leaf, ¾ teaspoon kosher salt, and ½ teaspoon pepper. Add the olive oil and blend just until the shallot is finely chopped. Transfer ⅓ cup (3 fl oz/80 ml) of the herb mixture to a large bowl.

Using a small, sharp knife or a vegetable peeler, peel a strip ½ inch (12 mm) wide around the center of each potato. Discard the peels and add the potatoes to the bowl with the herb mixture. Toss the potatoes to coat well.

Transfer the potatoes to the prepared baking sheet. Bake the potatoes, turning occasionally for even browning, until tender when pierced with a small knife and crusty brown, about 45 minutes. Transfer the potatoes to a large, shallow bowl. Drizzle with the remaining herb mixture and serve at once.

MAKES 4 SERVINGS

Nonstick olive-oil cooking spray

1 large shallot, coarsely chopped

1 tablespoon chopped fresh thyme

1 tablespoon chopped fresh sage

1 tablespoon chopped fresh oregano

1 large clove garlic, coarsely chopped

1 bay leaf, preferably Turkish, finely crumbled

Kosher salt and freshly ground pepper

½ cup (4 fl oz/125 ml) olive oil

16 red or white new potatoes, about 2 lb (1 kg) total weight, scrubbed and patted dry

POTATO GRATIN

2 large cloves garlic,
1 halved and 1 minced

3 tablespoons unsalted
butter, at room
temperature

1¼ cups (10 fl oz/310 ml)
whole milk

1 cup (8 fl oz/250 ml)
heavy (double) cream

Kosher salt and freshly
ground pepper

2 pinches of freshly grated
nutmeg

5 russet potatoes, about
2½ lb (1.25 kg) total
weight

Preheat the oven to 375°F (190°C). Rub an 8-inch (20-cm) square baking dish or other 8-cup (64–fl oz/2-l) baking dish with the cut sides of the garlic halves and discard the halves. Coat the inside of the dish with 1 tablespoon of the butter.

In a large pot, combine the milk, cream, minced garlic, 1 teaspoon kosher salt, ½ teaspoon pepper, nutmeg, and the remaining 2 tablespoons butter. Peel 1 of the potatoes and cut it into slices ⅛ inch (3 mm) thick. Add the potato slices to the milk mixture to prevent discoloration. Repeat with the remaining potatoes. Bring the milk mixture to a simmer over medium heat, stirring occasionally. Cover and cook for 3 minutes.

Using a slotted spoon, transfer the potatoes to the prepared dish, arranging the top layer of potatoes in an overlapping pattern if desired. Pour all of the milk mixture over the potatoes. Cover the dish with buttered aluminum foil, buttered side down.

Bake the gratin for 40 minutes, then uncover and bake until the potatoes are tender, the liquid bubbles thickly, and the top is brown and crusty, about 20 minutes longer. Remove from the oven and let stand for 10 minutes, then serve.

MAKES 6 SERVINGS

NUTMEG

In this classic gratin, use freshly grated nutmeg for its superior flavor. Whole nutmeg is the smooth, hard, brown oval seed of a tropical evergreen tree. For grating, use a specialized nutmeg grater with tiny rasps and usually a small compartment for storing a nutmeg or two. Alternatively, scrape the nutmeg over the finest rasps of a box grater-shredder.

LATKES WITH HOMEMADE APPLESAUCE

To make the applesauce, in a heavy saucepan, combine the apples, apple juice concentrate, and cinnamon stick. Bring to a boil over high heat. Reduce the heat to low, cover, and simmer, stirring occasionally, until the apples are very tender, about 25 minutes. Remove from the heat. Mash the apples coarsely with the back of a fork. Sweeten the applesauce with sugar to taste, adding 1 tablespoon at a time. Transfer to a serving bowl, cover, and refrigerate until cold, for at least 2 hours or up to 3 days.

Put 2 large baking sheets in the oven and preheat to 300°F (150°C). To make the latkes, using a food processor fitted with the coarse shredder blade, shred one-third of the potatoes with one-third of the onion. Repeat with another third of the potatoes and onion. Transfer to a large kitchen towel. Fit the food processor with the blade attachment and finely chop the remaining potatoes and onion. Transfer to the towel. Gather the towel tightly around the potato mixture and squeeze out as much liquid as possible.

Transfer the potato mixture to a large bowl. Add the eggs, flour, 1 ¼ teaspoons kosher salt, ¾ teaspoon pepper, and baking powder and stir until well blended.

In a large, heavy nonstick frying pan, heat ¼ cup (2 fl oz/60 ml) of the vegetable oil over medium-high heat. Drop 1 heaping tablespoon of batter per latke into the pan, spacing them well apart. Using a heatproof plastic spatula, flatten into 3-inch (7.5-cm) rounds. Cook until crisp and brown on the bottom, about 3 minutes. Turn and cook until crisp and brown on the second side, about 3 minutes. Transfer to the baking sheets in the oven to keep warm. Repeat with the remaining batter, leaving any accumulated liquid in the bowl and adding more oil to the pan as needed. Serve the latkes hot with the applesauce alongside.

MAKES 6 SERVINGS

FOR THE APPLESAUCE:

2 lb (1 kg) Golden Delicious apples, peeled, cored, and quartered, then cut into ¾-inch (2-cm) pieces

⅓ cup (3 fl oz/80 ml) thawed frozen apple juice concentrate

½ cinnamon stick

2–4 tablespoons (1–2 oz/30–60 g) sugar

FOR THE LATKES:

4 russet potatoes, about 2 lb (1 kg) total weight, peeled and cut into 1-inch (2.5-cm) cubes

1 very large yellow onion, about ¾ lb (375 g), cut into 1-inch (2.5-cm) cubes

2 large eggs, beaten

3 tablespoons all-purpose (plain) flour

Kosher salt and coarsely ground pepper

¾ teaspoon baking powder

⅔–¾ cup (5–6 fl oz/ 160–180 ml) vegetable oil

POMMES ANNA

Nonstick vegetable-oil cooking spray

About ½ cup (4 fl oz/ 125 ml) clarified butter *(far right)*, melted

10 red potatoes, about 2½ lb (1.25 kg) total weight, peeled, cut into slices ⅛ inch (3 mm) thick, and end slices discarded

Kosher salt and freshly ground pepper

Preheat the oven to 450°F (230°C). Spray a 9-inch (23-cm) metal pie pan with nonstick vegetable-oil cooking spray. Spoon 2 tablespoons of the clarified butter into the pan and tilt to coat. Place 1 potato slice in the center of the pan and overlap more slices in concentric circles around the first slice until the bottom of the pan is covered. Drizzle with 1 tablespoon clarified butter and sprinkle with a little kosher salt and pepper. Stand 1 potato slice against the side of the pan and overlap with more slices all around the side until covered. Repeat layering the potatoes in the center as above, drizzling each layer with 1 tablespoon of the clarified butter and sprinkling with kosher salt and pepper. (You should have 4 or 5 layers of potatoes.)

Drizzle any remaining butter over the top of the potatoes. If necessary, trim the potatoes standing against the side of the pan to be level with the potatoes in the center. Spray a sheet of aluminum foil with the cooking spray and cover the pan tightly with the foil, sprayed side down. Place the pan directly on a stove-top burner over high heat and cook for 1 minute (the butter will sizzle).

Bake the potatoes for 25 minutes. Uncover, press the top with a spatula to compact, and continue to bake, uncovered, until the potatoes are tender when pierced with a knife and the top and sides are very brown, about 30 more minutes.

Run a small knife around the pan sides to loosen the potato cake. Invert a flat plate on top of the pan and, using pot holders, hold the pan and plate together. Tilt them over a small bowl and pour off any excess butter. Still holding the pan and plate together, invert the pan and tap it to loosen the cake. Lift off the pan. If a darker cake is desired, slide it onto a small baking sheet and broil (grill) for 1–2 minutes. Cut into wedges to serve.

MAKES 6 SERVINGS

CLARIFIED BUTTER
Also called drawn butter, this is butter from which the milk solids have been removed. It has a high smoke point and won't burn easily, even when cooked over high heat. To make ⅔–¾ cup (5–6 fl oz/ 160–180 ml) clarified butter, bring 1 cup (8 oz/250 g) unsalted butter to a simmer in a small saucepan over medium heat. Remove from the heat and let stand for 3 minutes, then spoon off the foam and discard. Spoon the clear (clarified) liquid into a small glass jar and discard the milky sediment in the bottom of the pan. Cover and store in the refrigerator for up to 1 month.

POTATO-LEEK SOUP

RINSING LEEKS

Leeks are a flavorful, aromatic vegetable related to both onions and garlic. To prepare a leek, trim off the roots and cut off and discard the dark green tops, leaving only the white and pale green parts. (If a recipe specifies white part only, cut away all the green tops.) Halve the leek lengthwise, leaving the long layers attached at the root end. Hold the leek under cold running water, separating the layers to wash away any dirt. Drain, cut side down, on paper towels before slicing.

In a large, heavy pot, melt 3 tablespoons of the butter over medium-high heat. Add 4 cups (12 oz/375 g) of the leeks and the green onion bottoms and sauté until the leeks are wilted, about 4 minutes (do not let them brown). Add the potatoes and stir for 1 minute to coat.

Add the stock to the pot and bring to a boil. Reduce the heat to medium-low, cover, and simmer until the potatoes are very tender, about 25 minutes. Remove from the heat.

Ladle out 3 cups (24 fl oz/750 ml) of the soup (both solids and liquid) and purée in batches in a blender until smooth. Return the purée to the pot and season to taste with kosher salt and pepper.

To make a topping for the soup, in a small, heavy frying pan, melt the remaining 1 tablespoon butter over medium-low heat. Add the remaining leeks and 2 tablespoons of the green onion tops. (Reserve the remaining green tops for another use.) Sauté until the leeks wilt, about 4 minutes (do not let them brown). Season to taste with kosher salt and pepper.

Ladle the soup into warmed bowls and garnish each bowl with a dollop of sour cream, if desired. Sprinkle with the leek-and-onion topping and serve.

MAKES 4–6 SERVINGS

4 tablespoons (2 oz/60 g) unsalted butter

3 large leeks, including pale green parts, halved lengthwise, well rinsed, and thinly sliced (about 6 cups/18 oz/560 g)

3 green (spring) onions, green tops and white bottoms chopped separately

3 russet potatoes, about 1½ lb (750 g) total weight, peeled and diced

5 cups (40 fl oz/1.25 l) chicken stock (page 111) or canned low-sodium chicken broth

Kosher salt and freshly ground pepper

Sour cream, crème fraîche (page 113), or heavy (double) cream for garnish (optional)

FRENCH FRIES WITH HOMEMADE KETCHUP

FOR THE KETCHUP:

1 can (28 oz/875 g) tomato sauce

½ cup (4 fl oz/125 ml) red wine vinegar

2 large shallots, chopped

¼ cup (2 oz/60 g) sugar

1 tablespoon fennel seeds, crushed

1 teaspoon kosher salt

½ teaspoon ground cloves

¼ teaspoon dry mustard

¼ teaspoon coarsely ground black pepper

⅛ teaspoon cayenne pepper

FOR THE FRENCH FRIES:

4 large russet potatoes, about 2½ lb (1.25 kg) total weight

Vegetable oil for deep-frying

Kosher salt and freshly ground black pepper

To make the ketchup, in a large, heavy saucepan, combine the tomato sauce, red wine vinegar, shallots, sugar, fennel seeds, kosher salt, cloves, dry mustard, black pepper, and cayenne. Bring to a boil over medium heat, stirring occasionally. Reduce the heat to very low, cover, and simmer until the sauce thickens, about 30 minutes, stirring occasionally (and, during the last 10 minutes of cooking, often). Transfer the ketchup to a small bowl and let cool. Cover and refrigerate for at least 1 day or up to 3 weeks.

To make the French fries, peel the potatoes and cut each potato lengthwise into slices ⅓ inch (9 mm) thick. Cut the slices lengthwise into sticks ⅓ inch (9 mm) thick. Spread out 3 kitchen towels. Scatter the potatoes over the towels and roll them up. Let stand for 30 minutes to allow most of the moisture to be absorbed.

Pour vegetable oil to a depth of 2 inches (5 cm) into a large, heavy pot with a deep-frying thermometer attached to the side *(right)*. Heat the oil over medium-high heat until it registers 325°F (165°C). Working in 4 batches, fry the potatoes until just tender but not brown, about 3 minutes. Using a large skimmer, transfer the potatoes to a baking sheet lined with several layers of paper towels to drain. Between batches, let the oil return to 325°F and use the skimmer to remove any potato bits that remain in the oil. Let the potatoes cool for at least 1 hour or up to 3 hours.

Reheat the oil in the pot to 375°F (190°C). Fry the potatoes again in 4 batches until they are a deep golden brown and crisp, 3–4 minutes per batch. Transfer the potatoes to a baking sheet lined with fresh paper towels and sprinkle to taste with kosher salt and black pepper. Serve at once, with the ketchup.

Caution: When deep-frying, do not let the oil reach above 375°F (190°C). If it reaches 400°F (200°C) or more, it may burst into flame.

MAKES 6 SERVINGS

DEEP-FRYING SAVVY

If you do not have a deep fryer with a built-in thermometer, use a large, heavy pot and a deep-frying thermometer that can be clipped to the side. Never fill the pot more than one-third full of oil, and use an oil with a high smoke point, such as safflower, soybean, or peanut. Cook the food in small batches to prevent a drop in the oil temperature, using a skimmer to lower the food into the hot oil to avoid spatters. Always let the oil return to its correct frying temperature between batches. If the oil dips below that temperature, the French fries will absorb too much oil and become greasy.

DELMONICO POTATOES

SHALLOTS

A small member of the onion family, shallots look like large cloves of garlic covered in a papery bronze skin. They have white flesh lightly streaked with purple and a crisp texture. Shallots have a more subtle taste than onions, and for this reason they are used for flavoring dishes that may be overpowered by onion's strong flavor—such as this classic inspired by New York's Delmonico's Restaurant. Shallots should not be confused with scallions, which are long green (spring) onions with slender white bulbs.

Preheat the oven to 350°F (180°C). Butter an 11-by-7-inch (28-by-18-cm) baking dish or other 8-cup (64–fl oz/2-l) baking dish.

In a large pot of salted boiling water, cook the unpeeled whole potatoes until just tender when pierced with a small knife, about 25 minutes. Drain, let cool, and peel. Cut the potatoes into small dice. Transfer to a large bowl and add ½ teaspoon kosher salt and ¼ teaspoon black pepper. Toss to coat. Add 1 cup (4 oz/120 g) of the cheese and ½ cup (4 fl oz/125 ml) of the cream. Mix well.

In a small, heavy saucepan, melt 1 tablespoon of the butter over medium-low heat. Whisk in the flour, dry mustard, cloves, and cayenne and cook for 1 minute. Whisk in the milk and the remaining ½ cup cream. Raise the heat to medium-high and bring to a boil, whisking constantly, until slightly thickened, about 1 minute. Remove from the heat. Add ½ cup (2 oz/60 g) of the cheese, ¾ teaspoon kosher salt, and ¼ teaspoon black pepper and whisk until the cheese melts. Pour the sauce over the potatoes and stir to blend. Transfer to the prepared dish.

In a heavy frying pan, melt the remaining 2 tablespoons butter over medium heat. Add the shallot and summer savory and sauté until the shallot softens, about 3 minutes. Add the bread crumbs and stir until they are crisp and golden, about 7 minutes. Remove from the heat and let cool. Stir in the remaining ½ cup cheese and ¼ teaspoon black pepper. Set aside.

Bake the potatoes, uncovered, until the sauce is bubbling thickly and the potatoes are heated through, about 30 minutes. Sprinkle the crumb topping evenly over the potatoes. Continue to bake until the topping is crisp and the cheese is melted, about 10 minutes longer. Remove from the oven and let stand for 5 minutes before serving.

MAKES 6 SERVINGS

4 White Rose potatoes, about 1¾ lb (875 g) total weight, scrubbed

Kosher salt and freshly ground black pepper

2 cups (8 oz/240 g) firmly packed coarsely shredded extra-sharp Cheddar cheese

1 cup (8 fl oz/250 ml) heavy (double) cream

3 tablespoons unsalted butter, plus extra for greasing

1½ tablespoons all-purpose (plain) flour

¾ teaspoon dry mustard

⅛ teaspoon ground cloves

Pinch of cayenne pepper

1 cup (8 fl oz/250 ml) whole milk

1 large shallot, minced

1 teaspoon dried summer savory or thyme

2 cups (4 oz/125 g) fresh sourdough bread crumbs (page 44)

MASHED
ON THE SIDE

Warm and comforting, mashed potatoes are as appreciated in four-star restaurants as they are at family meals. They blend well with most flavors and textures, giving cooks the chance to stir in everything from roasted garlic to Brie cheese to sautéed greens, with delicious results. Traditionalists, of course, will be happy with nothing more than a simple pat of butter on top.

PERFECT MASHED POTATOES

To steam the potatoes, peel and cut them into rounds ¼ inch (6 mm) thick or into ½-inch (12-mm) dice. Pour water to a depth of 1 inch (2.5 cm) into a large pot and bring to a boil. Put the potatoes into a collapsible steamer basket and set the basket over the boiling water. (The water should not touch the bottom of the steamer basket.) Cover and steam until tender when pierced with a small knife, about 12 minutes. Transfer the potatoes to a bowl.

Alternatively, leave the potatoes whole and unpeeled and cook them in a large pot of salted boiling water until tender when pierced with a small knife, about 25 minutes. Transfer the potatoes to a colander to drain.

Empty the pot and wipe dry. Add the butter to the still-hot pot and let melt. Add the steamed potatoes to the pot or quickly peel the boiled potatoes while still hot (page 108) and add them to the pot. Mash with a potato masher until smooth.

Add ½ cup of the milk, 1½ teaspoons kosher salt, and ½ teaspoon pepper and mash to blend. Gradually add more milk, 1 tablespoon at a time, if needed to reach the desired consistency. Transfer the potatoes to a bowl and serve at once.

Note: Using a potato masher will yield slightly lumpy, fluffy mashed potatoes. For a smoother consistency, use a ricer. Do not use a food processor, or the potatoes will be gluey.

Make-Ahead Tip: The mashed potatoes can be prepared up to 2 hours in advance. Let stand in the pot at room temperature, then reheat gently over low heat, stirring often, just before serving. Alternatively, reheat in a buttered ovenproof dish in a 350°F (180°C) oven until crusty on top, about 25 minutes.

MAKES 6–8 SERVINGS

8 small russet or medium Yukon gold potatoes, about 3 lb (1.5 kg) total weight, scrubbed

½ cup (4 oz/125 g) unsalted butter, at room temperature

½–¾ cup (4–6 fl oz/ 125–180 ml) whole milk

Kosher salt and freshly ground pepper

ROASTED-GARLIC MASHED POTATOES

2 large heads garlic

2 tablespoons olive oil

5 large Yukon gold
potatoes, about 2½ lb
(1.25 kg) total weight,
peeled and cut into rounds
¼ inch (6 mm) thick

4 tablespoons (2 oz/60 g)
unsalted butter, at room
temperature

6 tablespoons (3 fl oz/
90 ml) whole milk, plus
more if needed

Kosher salt and freshly
ground pepper

Preheat the oven to 400°F (200°C). Cut a ½-inch (12-mm) slice off the top of each garlic head to expose the cloves, put the garlic in a small baking dish, and drizzle with the olive oil. Cover tightly with aluminum foil and bake until very tender when pierced with a small knife, about 55 minutes. Remove from the oven, uncover, and let cool to the touch. Break apart the garlic heads. Peel or squeeze each clove from its base to push out the garlic. In a small bowl, mash the garlic with a fork until almost smooth. You should have about ⅓ cup (3½ oz/105 g). Reserve any olive oil from the baking dish.

Pour water to a depth of 1 inch (2.5 cm) into a large pot and bring to a boil. Put the potatoes into a collapsible steamer basket and set the basket over the boiling water. (The water should not touch the bottom of the steamer basket.) Cover and steam until the potatoes are tender when pierced with a small knife, about 15 minutes. Transfer the potatoes to a bowl.

Empty the pot and wipe dry. Return the potatoes to the still-hot pot. Add the butter and 4 tablespoons of the roasted garlic and mash well with a potato masher. Add the 6 tablespoons milk, 1 teaspoon kosher salt, and ½ teaspoon pepper. Continue to mash, adding more milk, 1 tablespoon at a time, if needed to reach the desired consistency. Taste and add more of the roasted garlic, if desired. Serve at once, drizzled with the reserved garlic oil.

Note: There are so many delicious uses for roasted garlic (right) *that you may want to double the recipe, just to have leftovers. It will keep, covered and refrigerated, for up to 1 week.*

Make-Ahead Tip: These potatoes can be prepared up to 2 hours in advance. Cover loosely and let stand at room temperature, then reheat gently over low heat, stirring often, just before serving.

MAKES 4 SERVINGS

ROASTED GARLIC

Roasted garlic gives a depth of mellow flavor to mashed potatoes and can be added to a variety of other dishes. Mix it into mayonnaise to spread on roast beef sandwiches, add it to meat loaf or hamburgers, or mash and whisk it into gravy to thicken and season. For bruschetta, smear roasted garlic on toasted baguette slices and top with seasoned chopped tomatoes.

MASHED POTATOES
BAKED WITH THREE CHEESES

Preheat the oven to 350°F (180°C). Butter a 9-inch (23-cm) pie dish.

Pour water to a depth of 1 inch (2.5 cm) into a large pot and bring to a boil. Put the potatoes into a collapsible steamer basket and set the basket over the boiling water. (The water should not touch the bottom of the steamer basket.) Cover and steam until the potatoes are tender when pierced with a small knife, about 15 minutes. Transfer the potatoes to a bowl.

Empty the pot and wipe dry. Return the potatoes to the still-hot pot. Add two-thirds of the Brie cheese, two-thirds of the goat cheese, and two-thirds of the Parmesan cheese and mash well with a potato masher. Add the ¼ cup milk, a scant ¼ teaspoon kosher salt, and ¼ teaspoon pepper and mash to blend, adding more milk, 1 tablespoon at a time, if needed to reach the desired consistency. Transfer the potatoes to the prepared dish. Sprinkle the remaining cheeses evenly over the potatoes.

Bake the potatoes until heated through and the cheese is just beginning to brown on top, about 20 minutes. Serve at once, sprinkled with the parsley.

Make-Ahead Tip: This dish can be prepared up to 2 hours in advance. Cover loosely and let stand at room temperature until ready to bake.

Serving Tip: These mashed potatoes are very rich, so serve them with a simple main course such as grilled salmon, chicken, or lamb chops.

MAKES 6 SERVINGS

BRIE CHEESE

Sublimely smooth, ivory-colored Brie cheese is made from pasteurized or unpasteurized cow's milk. Most aficionados prefer the unpasteurized version, but it is rare outside of Europe. Brie is sold in flat rounds of various sizes. Its mild flavor, creamy texture, and buttery richness complement the other cheeses in this dish and make it a natural partner to mashed potatoes.

Unsalted butter for greasing

4 large russet potatoes, about 2 ½ lb (1.25 kg) total weight, peeled and cut into ½-inch (12-mm) cubes

4 ½ oz (140 g) Brie cheese, rind removed, cut into ½-inch (12-mm) dice

5 ½ oz (170 g) fresh white goat cheese, crumbled

¾ cup (2 ¼ oz/67 g) grated Parmesan cheese

¼ cup (2 fl oz/60 ml) whole milk, plus more if needed

Kosher salt and freshly ground pepper

2 tablespoons minced fresh flat-leaf (Italian) parsley

MASHED POTATOES
WITH PARSNIPS AND HORSERADISH

4 russet potatoes, about 2 lb (1 kg) total weight, peeled and cut into rounds ¼ inch (6 mm) thick

3 parsnips, about ¾ lb (375 g) total weight, peeled and cut into rounds ¼ inch (6 mm) thick

4 tablespoons (2 oz/60 g) unsalted butter, at room temperature

2 tablespoons prepared white cream-style horseradish

Kosher salt and freshly ground pepper

⅓ cup (3 fl oz/80 ml) half-and-half (half cream) or heavy (double) cream, plus more as needed

Pour water to a depth of 1 inch (2.5 cm) into a large pot and bring to a boil. Put the potatoes and parsnips into a collapsible steamer basket and set the basket over the boiling water. (The water should not touch the bottom of the steamer basket.) Cover and steam until the vegetables are very tender when pierced with a small knife, about 15 minutes. Transfer the potatoes and parsnips to a bowl.

Empty the pot and wipe dry. Return the vegetables to the still-hot pot. Add the butter, horseradish, 1 teaspoon kosher salt, and ¼ teaspoon pepper and mash with a potato masher until smooth. Add the ⅓ cup half-and-half and mash to blend, adding more half-and-half, 1 tablespoon at a time, if needed to reach the desired consistency. Transfer the potatoes to a bowl and serve immediately.

Make-Ahead Tip: This dish can be prepared up to 2 hours in advance. Cover loosely and let stand at room temperature, then reheat gently over low heat, stirring often, just before serving.

MAKES 4–6 SERVINGS

PARSNIPS

An underappreciated root vegetable, the parsnip looks like a white carrot and has a slightly sweet flavor. Parsnips can be cooked in the same way you cook carrots—boiled, steamed, roasted, or grilled. Unlike carrots, however, they are not good eaten raw. Try to buy them individually rather than in bags, since the bagged ones are often not as fresh and, once peeled, are usually too thin to be useful in many dishes. Parsnips are at their peak of flavor during the cold winter months when frost converts their starches to sugar.

COLCANNON

Pour water to a depth of 1 inch (2.5 cm) into a large pot and bring to a boil. Put the potatoes into a collapsible steamer basket and set the basket over the boiling water. (The water should not touch the bottom of the steamer basket.) Cover and steam until the potatoes are tender when pierced with a small knife, about 15 minutes. Transfer the potatoes to a bowl.

Empty the pot and wipe dry. Return the potatoes to the still-hot pot. Add ¼ cup (2 oz/60 g) of the butter, the milk, ¾ teaspoon kosher salt, and ¼ teaspoon pepper and mash well with a potato masher.

Melt the remaining ¼ cup butter in another large pot over medium heat. Add the leek and shallots and sauté until the vegetables begin to soften, about 5 minutes. Add the kale and toss just until wilted but still bright green, about 3 minutes. Add the napa cabbage and toss until tender-crisp, about 8 minutes. Sprinkle with the mace, ¼ teaspoon kosher salt, and ¼ teaspoon pepper. Cover and cook until the flavors blend, about 1 minute. Stir the cabbage mixture into the potatoes.

Reheat the potatoes over low heat, stirring often, about 5 minutes. Transfer to a bowl, sprinkle with the green onion, and serve.

Note: Colcannon, a dish of potatoes mashed with onions, cabbage, and kale is a mainstay of the Irish kitchen. This embellished version features three members of the onion family.

MAKES 6 SERVINGS

KALE

A dark green member of the cabbage family, kale has firm, tightly crinkled leaves and long stems. Both its earthy flavor and sturdy texture hold up well in cooking. Kale and other leafy greens may be very sandy, so rinse them well to wash away any grit. To remove the tough stems before cooking, fold the leaf in half lengthwise and strip or cut the stem away from the leaf along the folded edge. You can also use this technique to stem other greens such as Swiss chard and large spinach leaves.

5 russet potatoes, about 2½ lb (1.25 kg) total weight, peeled and cut into ½-inch (12-mm) cubes

½ cup (4 oz/120 g) unsalted butter, at room temperature

¼ cup (2 fl oz/60 ml) whole milk

Kosher salt and freshly ground pepper

1 large leek, including pale green parts, halved lengthwise and well rinsed (page 18), then thinly sliced

4 large shallots, thinly sliced

1 bunch kale, about 1 lb (500 g), well rinsed and stemmed *(far left)*, then coarsely chopped

1 head napa cabbage, about 1½ lb (750 g), cored and coarsely chopped

⅛ teaspoon ground mace or freshly grated nutmeg

⅔ cup (2 oz/60 g) chopped green (spring) onion tops

MASHED SWEET POTATOES
WITH BOURBON AND MOLASSES

6 small yams (orange-fleshed sweet potatoes), about 3 lb (1.5 kg) total weight, scrubbed and patted dry

4 tablespoons (2 oz/60 g) unsalted butter

3 tablespoons sugar

3 tablespoons light unsulfured molasses

3 tablespoons bourbon

Kosher salt and freshly ground pepper

⅛ teaspoon ground allspice

⅛ teaspoon freshly grated nutmeg

Preheat the oven to 400°F (200°C).

Prick each yam several times with a fork. Place the yams directly on an oven rack and bake until tender when pierced with a small knife, about 45 minutes. Alternatively, cook in a microwave on high heat for about 8 minutes. Turn the yams over and continue to cook until tender, about 10 minutes longer.

Cut the yams in half lengthwise. Scoop the flesh into a large saucepan and discard the skins. Add the butter, sugar, molasses, bourbon, ½ teaspoon kosher salt, ¼ teaspoon pepper, allspice, and nutmeg. Mash with a potato masher until smooth. Rewarm the yams over low heat, stirring often, about 5 minutes. Transfer the yams to a bowl and serve at once.

Make-Ahead Tip: This dish can be prepared up to 2 hours in advance. Cover loosely and let stand at room temperature, then reheat gently over low heat, stirring often, just before serving.

Serving Tip: Serve these Southern-style yams with fried chicken, chicken-fried steak, or blackened catfish fillets.

MAKES 4–6 SERVINGS

BOURBON

A type of whiskey that takes its name from a county in the state of Kentucky in the southern United States, bourbon is made from fermented grain, primarily corn. It is slightly sweet and pairs nicely with the molasses and yams in this recipe. Bourbon is a common cooking ingredient in the South, where it turns up in recipes for barbecue sauce, baked beans, cakes, and pies.

FROM THE OVEN

These baking and roasting recipes demonstrate that one of the best ways to cook potatoes is in the steady heat of the oven. Baked whole and stuffed with spinach and melted cheese, cut into thick slices roasted to a golden crisp, layered in a rich, bubbly gratin—no other vegetable can satisfy quite like the potato.

TWICE-BAKED POTATOES
WITH SPINACH AND CHEDDAR CHEESE

CHEDDAR CHEESE
Cheddar, first made in the village of Cheddar in England, is appreciated for its tangy, salty flavor, which ranges from mild to sharp, depending on age. Farmhouse Cheddars are stronger than other varieties. Although naturally a creamy white, Cheddar is often dyed orange with annatto, a paste made from achiote seeds. Other cheese-and-greens combinations that would be good in this recipe include fontina cheese and arugula (rocket), goat cheese and watercress, and Jack cheese and mustard greens.

Position a rack in the upper third of the oven and preheat to 400°F (200°C). Prick the potatoes with a fork and place them directly on the oven rack. Bake until tender when pierced with a small knife, about 1 hour. Remove from the oven and let cool for 5 minutes. Reduce the oven temperature to 350°F (180°C).

Meanwhile, in a large, heavy pot, melt 2 tablespoons of the butter over medium heat. Add the garlic and shallot and sauté until the shallot is translucent, about 3 minutes. Raise the heat to medium-high. Add the spinach and toss until wilted but still bright green, about 4 minutes. Using tongs, transfer the spinach mixture to a sieve set over a bowl. Using the back of a large spoon, press all the liquid out of the spinach.

Using a serrated knife, cut a lengthwise slice ½ inch (12 mm) thick off one long side of each potato and discard. Scoop out the potato flesh into a large bowl, leaving a shell ¼ inch (6 mm) thick. Add the sour cream, ½ teaspoon kosher salt, ¼ teaspoon pepper, and the remaining 4 tablespoons (2 oz/60 g) butter to the potato flesh and mash with a potato masher to blend. Stir in ⅔ cup (3 oz/90 g) of the cheese and then the spinach. Do not overmix; there should be streaks of spinach and cheese. Spoon the potato mixture into the potato shells, mounding it high. Press the remaining cheese on top of the filling, about 1 generous tablespoon for each potato.

Transfer the potatoes to a baking sheet and bake until heated through, about 20 minutes. To test for doneness, stick a small knife into a potato and leave it there for about 15 seconds. Remove the knife and feel the blade; if it is hot, the potato is too. Serve the potatoes at once.

MAKES 4 SERVINGS

4 large russet potatoes, about 2½ lb (1.25 kg) total weight, scrubbed and patted dry

6 tablespoons (3 oz/90 g) unsalted butter

2 large cloves garlic, minced

1 large shallot, minced

2 bunches fresh spinach leaves, well rinsed and tough stems removed (page 34)

2 tablespoons sour cream

Kosher salt and freshly ground pepper

1 cup (4 oz/125 g) firmly packed shredded extra-sharp Cheddar cheese

BAKED SWEET POTATOES
WITH GREEN CHILE BUTTER

FOR THE GREEN CHILE BUTTER:

2 tablespoons olive oil

2 large poblano chiles, about 9 oz (280 g) total weight, seeded and coarsely chopped

1 cup (1 oz/30 g) tightly packed fresh cilantro (fresh coriander) leaves

2 large green (spring) onions, including pale and dark green parts, chopped

3 large cloves garlic, chopped

2 green jalapeño chiles, seeded, deveined, and chopped

1 teaspoon dried oregano, preferably Mexican

Kosher salt and freshly ground pepper

½ cup (4 oz/125 g) unsalted butter, diced, at room temperature

2 teaspoons fresh lime juice

6 large sweet potatoes (tan-skinned), about 3¾ lb (1.85 kg) total weight, scrubbed and patted dry

To make the green chile butter, heat the olive oil over high heat in a frying pan. Add the poblano chiles and sauté until tender-crisp and beginning to blister but still bright green, about 5 minutes. Transfer the chiles to a bowl and let cool completely. In a food processor, combine the cilantro, green onions, garlic, jalapeño chiles, oregano, ½ teaspoon kosher salt, and a generous ¼ teaspoon pepper. Blend until finely chopped, scraping down the sides of the work bowl occasionally, about 30 seconds. Add the butter and lime juice and process until just blended. Add the poblano chiles and blend until the chiles are finely chopped. Set aside.

Preheat the oven to 400°F (200°C). Prick each sweet potato several times with a fork. Place the potatoes directly on an oven rack and bake until tender when pierced with a knife, about 45 minutes. Make a lengthwise vertical cut in one side of each sweet potato. Press in the sides to force the potatoes open. Spoon in a large dollop of the chile butter and serve.

Make-Ahead Tip: The chile butter can be made up to 1 week in advance, covered, and refrigerated. Before using, let it stand at room temperature until beginning to soften, about 1 hour.

Variation Tip: Try the chile butter on grilled salmon or chicken breasts. It is also wonderful spread on warm corn bread or tortillas.

MAKES 6 SERVINGS

GREEN CHILE VARIETIES
Fresh poblano chiles are large, dark green triangular-shaped chiles with a mild, rich flavor. Sometimes poblanos are erroneously labeled pasilla chiles in the market. (True pasillas are longer, narrower, and dark brown.) When dried, poblanos turn a deep reddish brown and are known as ancho chiles. Jalapeño chiles, also used here, are about 2 inches (5 cm) long, smooth, dark green (or bright red when ripe), and hot. For information on seeding and deveining chiles, see page 84.

ROASTED POTATO SLICES
WITH A ROSEMARY-GARLIC CRUST

FRESH BREAD CRUMBS

Fresh bread crumbs have delicate flavor and tender texture and make a crisp, light crust for potatoes. To make fresh crumbs, use day-old country-style bread. Cut off the crusts, tear the slices into bite-sized pieces, and process in a blender or food processor until finely ground. Store any extra crumbs in a zippered plastic bag in the refrigerator for up to 4 days.

In a large pot of salted boiling water, cook the unpeeled whole potatoes until just tender when pierced with a small knife, about 25 minutes. Drain and let cool, then refrigerate until cold, at least 2–3 hours or up to 1 day. Peel the potatoes and cut them lengthwise into slices ½ inch (12 mm) thick. Use the center 3 slices from each potato. (Reserve the remaining slices for another use.)

Preheat the oven to 400°F (200°C). Generously spray a large baking sheet with nonstick vegetable-oil cooking spray.

In a heavy frying pan, heat the olive oil over medium-low heat. Add the minced rosemary and garlic, cover, and cook until the garlic is softened but not brown, about 1 minute. Stir in the mustard, ½ teaspoon kosher salt, and ½ teaspoon pepper and remove from the heat. Add the bread crumbs and toss until evenly coated. Stir in the cheese.

Arrange the potato slices on a work surface. Brush the tops generously with the egg white. Spread 1 tablespoon of the crumb mixture on each slice and press to adhere and cover evenly. Place the slices, coated side down, on the prepared baking sheet. Brush the uncoated sides with egg white. Spread the remaining crumb mixture on the slices, pressing to adhere.

Bake the potato slices until the coating on the bottom is crusty, about 8 minutes. Carefully slide a thin metal spatula under each slice and turn it over. Bake until brown on the second side, about 5 minutes longer. Transfer the potato slices to a platter, garnish with rosemary sprigs, if desired, and serve.

MAKES 4 SERVINGS

Kosher salt and freshly ground pepper

4 large russet or White Rose potatoes, about 2½ lb (1.25 kg) total weight, scrubbed

Nonstick vegetable-oil cooking spray

2 tablespoons olive oil

1 tablespoon minced fresh rosemary, plus sprigs for garnish (optional)

1 tablespoon minced garlic

1 tablespoon Dijon mustard

1½ cups (3 oz/90 g) fresh sourdough bread crumbs (far left)

½ cup (1½ oz/45 g) firmly packed grated Parmesan cheese

1 large egg white, beaten until foamy

44

SPICED FINGERLING POTATOES

4 teaspoons ground cumin

1½ teaspoons sweet Hungarian paprika

1½ teaspoons kosher salt

1 teaspoon freshly ground black pepper

½ teaspoon cayenne pepper

½ teaspoon garlic powder

¼ teaspoon ground cloves

1½ cups (12 oz/375 g) plain whole-milk yogurt

2½ tablespoons olive oil

2 lb (1 kg) fingerling potatoes *(far right)*, scrubbed and patted dry

Nonstick olive-oil cooking spray

¼ cup (⅓ oz/10 g) finely shredded or chopped fresh mint

In a small bowl, combine the cumin, paprika, kosher salt, black pepper, cayenne, garlic powder, and cloves. Stir to blend well. Set this mixture aside.

In a bowl, combine the yogurt and 2 teaspoons of the spice mixture to make a dipping sauce. Stir to blend. Cover and refrigerate for at least 2 hours or up to 2 days.

Put the olive oil in a large bowl and stir in the remaining spice mixture. Cut 2 or 3 shallow lengthwise slits in the sides of each potato to allow the seasonings to penetrate. Add the potatoes to the bowl and toss to coat evenly.

Preheat the oven to 350°F (180°C). Spray a large, heavy baking sheet with nonstick olive-oil cooking spray. Arrange the potatoes on the prepared sheet, spacing them so that they do not touch. Roast the potatoes for about 30 minutes. Using tongs, carefully turn over the potatoes. Continue to roast until the potatoes are tender and browned, about 25 minutes longer.

Put the bowl of yogurt dipping sauce in the center of a serving platter. Arrange the potatoes around the sauce, sprinkle them with the mint, and serve.

Make-Ahead Tip: The potatoes can be dressed with the spice mixture up to 4 hours in advance. Let stand at room temperature, tossing occasionally, before baking.

MAKES 4 SERVINGS

FINGERLING POTATOES

Certain potato varieties are called fingerlings because of the narrow, fingerlike shape of the tubers. Russian Banana is among the most widely available. Other varieties include La Ratte, Rose Finn Apple, and Ruby Crescent. If you can't find fingerling potatoes, baby red or white creamers are delicious alternatives.

FENNEL AND PARMESAN SCALLOPED POTATOES

FENNEL

Also known as sweet fennel or finocchio, fennel has a sweet, faintly aniselike flavor. The stems swell and overlap at the base of the plant to form a bulb with white to pale green ribbed layers that are similar to celery in appearance and texture. The feathery fronds slightly resemble fresh dill. Choose fennel bulbs that are smooth and tightly layered, with no cracks or bruises. When preparing fennel, cut off the tops. Then discard the outer layer of the bulb if it is tough and cut away any discolored areas.

Preheat the oven to 400°F (200°C). Butter an 8-inch (20-cm) square baking dish.

In a large pot, combine the cream, milk, chives, tarragon, thyme, 1 teaspoon kosher salt, and ½ teaspoon pepper. Add the potatoes and stir to coat.

Cut the fennel bulb into quarters lengthwise and slice thinly. Add 2 cups (6 oz/185 g) of the sliced fennel to the pot. Chop the reserved fronds and add 2 tablespoons to the pot.

Bring the potato mixture to a boil over medium-high heat, stirring occasionally. Boil for 1 minute. Using a slotted spoon, transfer half of the mixture to the prepared dish. Sprinkle evenly with half of the cheese. Top with the remaining potato mixture. Pour the remaining liquid from the pot over the potatoes. Sprinkle evenly with the remaining cheese. Cover the dish with buttered aluminum foil, buttered side down.

Bake the potatoes for about 40 minutes. Uncover and continue to bake until the potatoes are very tender, the cream is bubbling and reduced to a thick sauce, and the top is browned, about 20 minutes longer. Let stand for 10 minutes, then serve.

MAKES 6–8 SERVINGS

Unsalted butter for greasing

1½ cups (12 fl oz/375 ml) heavy (double) cream

1 cup (8 fl oz/250 ml) whole milk

¼ cup (⅓ oz/10 g) chopped fresh chives

1 tablespoon chopped fresh tarragon

1 teaspoon chopped fresh thyme

Kosher salt and freshly ground pepper

5 small russet potatoes, about 2 lb (1 kg) total weight, peeled and cut into rounds ⅛ inch (3 mm) thick

1 fennel bulb, trimmed, fronds reserved

1 cup (3 oz/90 g) firmly packed grated Parmesan cheese

APRICOT-GLAZED SWEET POTATO GRATIN

2¾ cups (22 fl oz/685 ml) apricot nectar

2 tablespoons sugar

Kosher salt and freshly ground pepper

Large pinch of ground allspice

3 small yams (orange-fleshed sweet potatoes), about 1½ lb (750 g) total weight

2 sweet potatoes (tan-skinned), about 1 lb (500 g) total weight

6 tablespoons (3 fl oz/ 90 ml) heavy (double) cream, plus extra for drizzling

1 tablespoon unsalted butter, cut into bits, plus extra for greasing

3 tablespoons minced fresh chives

Preheat the oven to 400°F (200°C). Generously butter an 8-inch (20-cm) square baking dish.

In a large frying pan, combine the apricot nectar, sugar, ¾ teaspoon kosher salt, ⅛ teaspoon pepper, and allspice and stir to blend. Peel 1 of the yams and cut crosswise into rounds ¼ inch (6 mm) thick. Add to the pan and stir to coat. Repeat with the remaining yams and the sweet potatoes.

Bring the mixture to a boil over medium-high heat. Reduce the heat to medium-low, cover, and simmer, stirring occasionally, until the yams and sweet potatoes begin to soften, about 8 minutes. Remove from the heat. Using a slotted spoon, transfer the yams and sweet potatoes to the prepared dish. (If desired, overlap the top layer of yams and sweet potatoes in a decorative pattern.) Set aside.

Return the liquid in the frying pan to medium-high heat and add the 6 tablespoons (3 fl oz/90 ml) cream. Boil, stirring occasionally, to reduce the liquid to 1½ cups (12 fl oz/375 ml), about 10 minutes. Pour the liquid evenly over the yams and sweet potatoes. Dot the surface with the bits of butter.

Bake the gratin, uncovered, until the yams and sweet potatoes are very tender, the top is deep brown in places, and the liquid is almost absorbed, about 1 hour. Remove from the oven and let stand for 15 minutes. Serve, drizzled with cream and sprinkled generously with the chives.

MAKES 6 SERVINGS

SWEET POTATOES

Sweet potatoes are the edible roots of a plant from the morning glory family. Some have tan skin and pale yellow flesh and a mealy, dry, and fluffy texture when cooked. Others have dark reddish or purplish skin and deep orange flesh and a soft, moist texture and sweet flavor when cooked. The latter is known in the United States as a yam, although it is not a true yam, which is a different species from the sweet potato. True yams are an important crop in many countries but are rarely available in the United States.

POTATO, HAM, AND GRUYÈRE TART

On a lightly floured surface, roll out the pastry dough into a 13-inch (33-cm) round. Transfer the round to a 9-inch (23-cm) tart pan with a removable bottom. Trim the overhang to ¼ inch (6 mm) and fold the overhang in, making double-thick sides. (Creating a double thickness reinforces the sides of the pastry shell and also raises the sides slightly above the pan rim, to contain the filling better.) Prick the dough all over with a fork. Refrigerate the tart shell for 30 minutes.

Blind bake the shell *(left)*. Let cool on a wire rack. Lower the oven temperature to 375°F (190°C).

To make the filling, in a pot of salted boiling water, cook the unpeeled whole potato until tender when pierced with a small knife, about 30 minutes. Drain and let cool. Peel and cut into ⅓-inch (9-mm) cubes.

In a heavy frying pan, melt the butter over medium-high heat. Add the shallots and thyme and sauté until the shallots are translucent, about 2 minutes. Add 1 cup (5 oz/155 g) of the potato cubes (reserve the remainder for another use). Stir the potato cubes to coat with the shallot mixture, about 1 minute. Remove from the heat and stir in the ham.

In a small bowl, beat together the cream, egg, ¼ teaspoon kosher salt, ¼ teaspoon pepper, and nutmeg.

Spread the potato mixture evenly in the crust. Sprinkle with the cheese and pour the cream mixture evenly over the top. Bake the tart until the top begins to brown and the center is set, about 15 minutes. Remove from the oven and let cool on a wire rack for 15 minutes. Gently push the bottom of the pan up to loosen the tart from the pan sides. Place the tart (still on the pan bottom) onto a serving plate. Serve warm or at room temperature.

MAKES 4–6 SERVINGS

BLIND BAKING

Also called prebaking, blind baking means partially or completely baking a pie or tart shell before filling it. To bake partially (as in this recipe), preheat the oven to 425°F (220°C). Lay a sheet of foil over the chilled pastry in the pan. Fit the foil into the pan, completely covering the pastry, and fill with pie weights (above) or dried beans. Bake until the sides are set but not colored, about 15 minutes. Remove from the oven and remove the weights and foil. Return the shell to the oven and continue to bake until pale golden, pricking any bubbles with a fork, about 8 minutes longer.

1 recipe Pastry Dough, chilled (page 110)

FOR THE FILLING:

Kosher salt and freshly ground pepper

1 russet potato, about ½ lb (250 g), scrubbed

1 tablespoon unsalted butter

2 shallots, minced

½ teaspoon minced fresh thyme

3½ oz (105 g) trimmed Black Forest ham, cut into ⅓-inch (9-mm) dice (about ¾ cup)

½ cup (4 fl oz/125 ml) plus 2 tablespoons heavy (double) cream

1 large egg

Large pinch of freshly grated nutmeg

⅔ cup (2½ oz/75 g) firmly packed shredded Gruyère cheese

POTATO FOCACCIA WITH OLIVES AND FIGS

3 cups (24 fl oz/750 ml) water

1 large russet potato, about 10 oz (315 g), peeled and cut into ½-inch (12-mm) cubes

1 tablespoon honey

1 package (2½ teaspoons) active dry yeast

2 tablespoons extra-virgin olive oil, plus extra for drizzling (optional)

Kosher salt

About 3¾ cups (19 oz/ 590 g) all-purpose (plain) flour

¼ lb (125 g) Kalamata olives, pitted (page 73) and coarsely chopped (about ¾ cup)

¼ lb (125 g) dried Calimyrna figs, stemmed and coarsely chopped (about ¾ cup)

2 tablespoons whole coriander seeds, toasted (page 115)

In a small, heavy saucepan, bring the water to a boil over high heat. Add the potato and cook until tender, about 12 minutes. Using a slotted spoon, transfer the potato to a shallow bowl, reserving the potato cooking water. Pour 1 cup (8 fl oz/250 ml) of the potato water into a food processor and add the honey. Let stand until just warm (115°F/46°C), about 20 minutes. Discard the remaining potato water. Sprinkle the yeast over the water in the processor. Let stand until foamy, about 8 minutes.

Mash the potato with a potato masher and measure out ⅔ cup (5 oz/155 g). Add the measured mashed potato, 1 tablespoon of the olive oil, and 1½ teaspoons kosher salt to the food processor. Process until blended, about 5 seconds. Add 3 cups (15 oz/470 g) of the flour and process until moist clumps form. Add the olives and figs and pulse 6 times. Stir the dough with a spatula to help distribute the olives and figs and pulse 6 more times.

Sprinkle ¼ cup (1½ oz/45 g) of the flour on a work surface. Turn the dough out onto the surface and turn to coat with the flour. Knead gently until smooth, adding more flour as needed, about 3 minutes. Shape into a ball, cover, and let rest for 30 minutes.

Sprinkle a heavy 18-by-12-inch (45-by-30-cm) baking sheet with 3 tablespoons flour. Transfer the dough to the prepared sheet. Press and stretch the dough until almost the size of the sheet and brush with the remaining 1 tablespoon oil. Press the dough all over with your fingertips to dimple it. Sprinkle with the coriander seeds and ¾ teaspoon kosher salt. Cover loosely with a kitchen towel and let rise until light and puffy, about 1 hour.

Preheat the oven to 400°F (200°C). Bake until browned, about 20 minutes. Transfer to a rack and let cool for 15 minutes. Drizzle with olive oil if desired and serve warm or at room temperature.

MAKES 8–10 SERVINGS

YEAST

Yeast is the living substance that leavens bread. It eats the sugars in a dough and releases carbon dioxide bubbles that expand and "raise" the dough. To ensure that the yeast is alive and will leaven the dough, it should be proofed. To proof yeast, let the granules dissolve in warm water to which you've added a pinch of sugar or a little honey as food for the yeast. The yeast will become foamy. Use active dry yeast, not instant or quick-rise, for the best results in this recipe.

MAIN COURSES

An everyday vegetable admired for its staying power, the potato is a natural choice for main courses. Its neutral flavor makes it so easy to pair with other ingredients that the possibilities for delicious combinations are almost infinite. But the primary appeal of the potato remains in its role as an unequaled comfort food—familiar, satisfying, and restorative.

POTATO GNOCCHI WITH PESTO

To make the gnocchi, in a large pot of salted boiling water, cook the unpeeled whole potatoes until tender when pierced with a small knife, about 30 minutes. Drain and let cool. Peel the potatoes and place them in a large bowl. Add the Parmesan cheese, 1¼ teaspoons kosher salt, and nutmeg and mash well with a potato masher. Let cool to lukewarm, mix in the egg and then 1 cup (5 oz/155 g) of the flour. Knead the dough, adding more flour 1 tablespoonful at a time as needed, until a smooth, soft, and slightly sticky dough forms, about 3 minutes. Let the dough rest for 5 minutes, then divide it into 6 equal pieces. On a lightly floured surface, use your palms to roll each piece into a rope ¾ inch (2 cm) thick. Cut the ropes into 1-inch (2.5-cm) pieces. To form the gnocchi, roll each piece over the tines of a large fork or down the length of a wire whisk to create grooves.

In a large pot of generously salted boiling water, cook the haricots verts until tender-crisp, about 3 minutes. Using a skimmer, transfer the beans to a colander and drain.

In 2 batches, cook the gnocchi in the same pot of boiling water until just tender, stirring often to prevent sticking, about 5 minutes per batch. Using the skimmer, transfer to a baking sheet.

Put the pesto and the grated Parmesan cheese in a large bowl. In a large frying pan, melt the butter over medium-high heat. Add the gnocchi and sauté until heated through, about 5 minutes. Add the haricots verts and toss for 1 minute. Transfer the gnocchi and haricots verts to the bowl of pesto and cheese and toss to coat.

Divide among 4 individual plates. If desired, garnish with Parmesan shavings and basil leaves and drizzle with cream. Serve immediately.

MAKES 4 SERVINGS

PESTO
In a food processor, combine ½ cup (1½ oz/45 g) grated Parmesan cheese; 1 large clove garlic, halved; ½ teaspoon kosher salt; and ¼ teaspoon pepper. Process until the garlic is minced. Add 2 cups (2 oz/60 g) firmly packed fresh basil leaves and ¼ cup (1 oz/30 g) toasted pine nuts (page 115) and process until the basil is finely ground. With the motor running, gradually add ½ cup (4 fl oz/125 ml) olive oil and blend until almost smooth. Transfer to a small bowl, cover, and refrigerate. To keep for up to 1 week, spoon additional oil over the pesto to cover by ¼ inch (6 mm).

FOR THE GNOCCHI:

Kosher salt

3 russet potatoes, about 1½ lb (750 g) total weight, scrubbed

2 tablespoons grated Parmesan cheese

⅛ teaspoon freshly grated nutmeg

1 large egg, beaten

1¼ cups (6½ oz/200 g) all-purpose (plain) flour, plus more as needed

6 oz (185 g) haricots verts or other small, slender green beans, trimmed

½ cup (4 fl oz/125 ml) Pesto (far left)

½ cup (1½ oz/45 g) grated Parmesan cheese, plus shavings for garnish (optional)

6 tablespoons (3 oz/90 g) unsalted butter

Fresh basil leaves for garnish (optional)

Heavy (double) cream for drizzling (optional)

MASHED-POTATO BLINTZES

FOR THE BLINTZES:

1½ cups (12 fl oz/375 ml) water

4 large eggs

1 tablespoon sugar

Kosher salt

1½ cups (7½ oz/235 g) all-purpose (plain) flour

Vegetable oil for brushing

FOR THE FILLING:

4 large russet potatoes, about 2½ lb (1.25 kg) total weight

3 tablespoons sour cream

2 tablespoons unsalted butter

Kosher salt and freshly ground pepper

1 large egg, beaten

Caramelized Onions (far right)

About ½ cup (4 fl oz/ 125 ml) vegetable oil

Sour cream for serving

To make the blintzes, in a blender, combine the water, eggs, sugar, 1 teaspoon kosher salt, and ½ cup (2½ oz/75 g) of the flour. Blend until smooth. Add the remaining flour in 2 batches, blending after each addition. Let stand at room temperature for 1–2 hours.

Heat a 10-inch (25-cm) nonstick frying pan over medium-high heat. Brush with vegetable oil. Pour in 3 tablespoons batter and immediately tilt the pan, to cover the bottom evenly. Cook until the edges begin to brown and curl, about 45 seconds. Turn the blintz out onto a paper towel–lined plate and top with another paper towel. Repeat to cook the remaining batter, brushing the pan with oil each time and stacking the blintzes between paper towels. You should have twelve 7- to 8-inch (18- to 20-cm) blintzes.

Bake the potatoes as directed on page 111. Cut them in half and scoop the flesh into a large bowl. Add the sour cream and butter and mash well. Season with kosher salt and pepper. Let cool to lukewarm and mix in the egg.

Put 1 blintz on a work surface, cooked side up. Spoon 3 tablespoons of the mashed potatoes into a 3-inch (7.5-cm) log just below the center of the blintz. Top with a tablespoonful of the caramelized onions. Fold the bottom over the filling and fold in the sides. Roll up the blintz, enclosing the filling. Repeat with the remaining blintzes, reserving any remaining onions for garnish.

Divide the ½ cup vegetable oil between 2 large, nonstick frying pans and heat over medium heat. Add the blintzes to the pans, seam sides down. Cover and cook until brown and crisp on the bottom, about 5 minutes. Uncover, turn the blintzes over, and continue to cook until brown on the bottom and heated through, about 5 minutes. Place 2 blintzes each on individual plates. Serve hot, spooning additional sour cream and the reserved onions on top.

MAKES 6 SERVINGS

CARAMELIZED ONIONS

Vegetables such as onions, beets, and carrots can be caramelized by long cooking. This allows their natural sugars to develop a less purely sweet and more complex flavor. To make enough caramelized onions for this recipe, halve and thinly slice 2½ lb (1.25 kg) yellow onions. In a large frying pan, heat ¼ cup (2 fl oz/60 ml) vegetable oil over medium heat. Add the onions and sauté, stirring frequently, until deep brown, about 30 minutes. Sprinkle to taste with kosher salt and pepper and sauté 3 minutes longer. Let cool before using.

LAMB AND WILD MUSHROOM SHEPHERD'S PIE

CLEANING MUSHROOMS

Most mushrooms sold in the market today are already quite clean, but you may still need to attend to them a bit at home. Gently brushing mushrooms with a damp cloth or soft brush, such as a mushroom brush or pastry brush, is preferable to washing them. Porous mushrooms will soak up water like a sponge, compromising both the texture and flavor of any dish. Do not scrub so hard that you remove the thin outer skin on the caps; you want only to loosen any dirt or grit. Be sure to rinse the bristles on the brush if they begin to get soiled.

Preheat the oven to 350°F (180°C). To make the filling, cut the lamb into ½-inch (12-mm) pieces and stem and cut the mushrooms into ¾-inch (2-cm) pieces. In a large bowl, mix together the flour, ¾ teaspoon kosher salt, ½ teaspoon pepper, and allspice. Add the lamb and toss to coat evenly. In a large nonstick frying pan, heat 2 tablespoons of the olive oil over medium-high heat. Add the lamb and sauté until well browned, about 10 minutes. Transfer to a bowl. Add the remaining 1 tablespoon olive oil to the pan. Add the shallots and garlic and stir over medium-high heat for 1 minute. Add the mushrooms and bay leaf and sauté until well browned, about 6 minutes.

Return the lamb to the frying pan, stir in the stock and tomato paste, and bring to boil. Reduce the heat to medium-low, cover, and simmer until the lamb is tender, about 45 minutes. Uncover and simmer until the juices thicken, about 2 minutes. Transfer the filling to a 9-inch (23-cm) pie dish.

To make the topping, pour water to a depth of 1 inch (2.5 cm) into a large pot and bring to a boil. Peel and slice the potatoes into rounds ¼ inch (6 mm) thick. Put the potato slices into a collapsible steamer basket and set the basket over the boiling water. (The water should not touch the bottom of the steamer basket.) Cover and steam until tender when pierced with a small knife, about 12 minutes. Transfer the potatoes to a large bowl. Add the milk, butter, ½ teaspoon kosher salt, and pepper to taste. Mash well with a potato masher. Stir in half of the chives. Spoon the potatoes on top of the lamb mixture to cover it completely.

Bake the pie until it is heated through and the potatoes just begin to brown, about 35 minutes. Sprinkle with the remaining chives and serve.

MAKES 4 SERVINGS

FOR THE FILLING:

2 lb (1 kg) shoulder blade lamb chops, trimmed of fat and boned

1 lb (500 g) assorted wild mushrooms such as cremini, portobello, and shiitake

2 tablespoons all-purpose (plain) flour

Kosher salt and freshly ground pepper

½ teaspoon ground allspice

3 tablespoons olive oil

3 large shallots, minced

3 large cloves garlic, minced

1 Turkish bay leaf (page 10), minced

1¾ cups (14 fl oz/430 ml) beef stock (page 111)

1 tablespoon tomato paste

FOR THE TOPPING:

6 small Yukon gold potatoes, 1½ lb (750 g) total weight

⅓ cup (3 fl oz/80 ml) whole milk

4 tablespoons (2 oz/60 g) unsalted butter

Kosher salt and freshly ground pepper

¼ cup (⅓ oz/10 g) chopped fresh chives

POTATO GALETTES WITH SMOKED SALMON

4 russet potatoes, about 2 lb (1 kg) total weight

8 tablespoons (4 oz/125 g) unsalted butter, melted

10 tablespoons (1 oz/30 g) minced fresh chives, plus whole chives for garnish

Nonstick vegetable-oil cooking spray

1 cup (8 oz/250 g) crème fraîche (page 113) or sour cream

Kosher salt and freshly ground pepper

8 oz (240 g) thinly sliced smoked salmon

Preheat the oven to 425°F (220°C). Peel 1 potato. Using the large shredding holes of a box grater-shredder, shred into a bowl lined with a double thickness of paper towels. Squeeze the potato dry in the paper towels and return the potato to the bowl. Add 1 tablespoon of the melted butter and 1 tablespoon of the minced chives. Toss to mix well.

Spray a heavy 10-inch (25-cm) nonstick frying pan with nonstick vegetable-oil cooking spray. Add ½ tablespoon of the butter and heat over medium heat. Add the potato mixture. Using a heatproof plastic spatula, press the potato into a flat round 7 inches (18 cm) in diameter. Cook, pressing occasionally with the spatula, until the bottom is light brown, about 5 minutes. Loosen the galette and slide it out onto a plate. Top with another plate and invert. Heat ½ tablespoon butter in the same pan. Slide the galette back into the pan, cooked side up. Press flat with the spatula and cook until light brown on the second side, about 5 minutes. Slide the galette onto a large baking sheet. Repeat with the remaining 3 potatoes, preparing them one at a time, to make 3 more galettes.

Mix the crème fraîche and the remaining 6 tablespoons (½ oz/15 g) chives in a small bowl to blend. Set aside.

Bake the galettes for 5 minutes. Turn them over and continue to bake until crisp and deep brown, about 6 minutes longer. Transfer the galettes to individual plates. Sprinkle with kosher salt and pepper to taste. Top each galette with 2 oz (60 g) sliced smoked salmon and the chive crème fraîche. Garnish each galette with whole chives and serve.

MAKES 4 SERVINGS

SMOKED SALMON

Smoked salmon is always a delicacy. The variety recommended for use in this recipe is Irish- or Scotch-smoked salmon, two types of cold-smoked Atlantic salmon. In cold smoking, the fish is rubbed with a seasoning, dry-cured, and smoked at temperatures of 70°–90°F (21°–32°C) for periods of 1 day or up to a few weeks, depending on the smokiness desired. Lox from Jewish delicatessens is also cold smoked, after brining. It is often saltier than these other smoked salmons, but would also work in this recipe.

POTATO PIEROGI WITH
BRAISED RED CABBAGE AND FETA CHEESE

Bake the potatoes as directed on page 111. Alternatively, cook the potatoes in the microwave on high heat until tender, about 4 minutes per side. Remove from the oven and let cool for 5 minutes. Cut the potatoes in half and scoop the flesh out into a large bowl. Add ¾ cup (3 oz/90 g) of the feta cheese, the yogurt, and ¼ teaspoon pepper. Mash well. Stir in the egg yolk until blended.

While the potatoes are baking, make the cabbage. In a large, heavy frying pan, melt the butter over medium heat. Add the caraway seeds and sauté until fragrant, about 1 minute. Add the cabbage and onion and sauté until tender, about 10 minutes. Stir in the jelly, vinegar, ½ teaspoon kosher salt, and ¼ teaspoon pepper. Simmer until the juices thicken, about 5 minutes. Set aside.

To make the pierogi, line a baking sheet with waxed paper or parchment (baking) paper. In a small bowl, beat the egg white until foamy. Put a gyoza wrapper on a work surface. Brush the gyoza surface with egg white and place 1 level tablespoon potato filling in the center. Fold the wrapper over, making a half-circle, and press the edges together to seal. Place on the prepared baking sheet. Repeat with the remaining gyoza wrappers, egg white, and filling.

In a large pot of salted boiling water, cook the pierogi until tender, about 5 minutes. Drain well. Melt the butter in a large frying pan over medium heat and set aside. Add the pierogi to the pan with the melted butter and sauté over medium-high heat until they begin to brown, about 5 minutes.

Meanwhile, reheat the red cabbage over medium heat for 5 minutes. Divide among 4 individual plates or large shallow bowls. Spoon the pierogi around the cabbage, sprinkle with pepper and the remaining cheese, and serve.

MAKES 4 SERVINGS

GYOZA WRAPPERS
Gyoza wrappers are thin rounds of dough used to make Japanese dumplings. They resemble Chinese wonton or pot-sticker wrappers and are sold in the refrigerated deli section of most well-stocked supermarkets. Traditionally, pierogi are made with homemade, hand-rolled noodle dough, but purchased wrappers are a convenient and workable substitute. Square wonton wrappers can be used if the round wrappers are difficult to find.

2 russet potatoes, about 1 lb (500 g) total weight

5 oz (155 g) feta cheese, crumbled (about 1¼ cups)

2 tablespoons plain whole-milk yogurt

Freshly ground pepper

1 large egg, separated

FOR THE CABBAGE:

2 tablespoons unsalted butter

1 teaspoon caraway seeds

1 small red cabbage, about 1 lb (500 g), cored and very thinly sliced (about 6 cups)

½ red onion, very thinly sliced

2 tablespoons apple jelly or crabapple jelly

1 tablespoon cider vinegar

Kosher salt and freshly ground pepper

24 gyoza wrappers *(far left)*

6 tablespoons (3 oz/90 g) unsalted butter

POTATO, SMOKED TROUT, AND LEEK CROQUETTES

FOR THE TARTAR SAUCE:

½ cup (4 fl oz/125 ml)
mayonnaise

½ cup (4 oz/125 g) sour
cream

1 tablespoon drained
capers, chopped

1 tablespoon chopped
cornichons

1 tablespoon chopped fresh
tarragon

1 tablespoon white wine
tarragon vinegar

FOR THE CROQUETTES:

3 large russet potatoes,
about 2 lb (1 kg) total weight

1 large leek

8 tablespoons (4 oz/125 g)
unsalted butter

2 teaspoons minced fresh
tarragon

Kosher salt and freshly
ground pepper

6 oz (185 g) smoked trout
fillets, flaked

2 large eggs

2 cups (4 oz/120 g) fresh
French bread crumbs (from
about 6 slices) (page 44)

½ cup (2½ oz/75 g)
all-purpose (plain) flour

To make the tartar sauce, combine the mayonnaise, sour cream, capers, cornichons, tarragon, and tarragon vinegar in a small bowl and blend well. Cover and refrigerate.

Bake the potatoes as directed on page 111. Alternatively, cook the potatoes in the microwave on high heat until tender, 6–8 minutes per side. Remove from the oven and let cool for 5 minutes. Cut the potatoes in half and scoop the flesh out into a large bowl. Mash well with a potato masher. Measure 1½ cups (12 oz/375 g) mashed potatoes and transfer to a large bowl. (Reserve the remaining mashed potatoes for another use.)

Rinse the leek (page 18) and slice thinly, including the pale green parts. In a small frying pan, melt 2 tablespoons of the butter over medium heat. Add the leek and sauté until very tender, about 5 minutes. Add the leek to the mashed potatoes. Stir in the tarragon, ½ teaspoon kosher salt, and ¼ teaspoon pepper. Stir in the trout, then mix in 1 of the eggs and ½ cup (1 oz/30 g) of the bread crumbs. To form the croquettes, divide the mixture into 4 equal portions and shape each portion into a patty ¾ inch (2 cm) thick.

Place the flour, the remaining egg, and the remaining 1½ cups (3 oz/90 g) bread crumbs in separate shallow bowls. Using a fork, beat the egg well. Coat each croquette with the flour, then the egg, and then the bread crumbs, pressing to adhere.

In a large, heavy frying pan, melt the remaining 6 tablespoons (3 oz/90 g) butter over medium heat. Add the croquettes and cook turning once, until crisp, brown, and heated through, about 6 minutes per side. Transfer the croquettes to a platter or individual plates and serve accompanied with the tartar sauce.

Serving Tip: If desired, top each croquette with a small dollop of the tartar sauce, extra smoked salmon, and a sprig of fresh tarragon.

MAKES 4 SERVINGS

TARRAGON

An herb with a bright, assertive anise flavor, tarragon is especially prized in French cooking. Easy to recognize with its slender, pointed dark green leaves, fresh tarragon is most available in the summer and early autumn. If it is not available fresh, dried leaf tarragon (unlike many dried herbs) can fill in quite admirably.

TORTILLA ESPAÑOLA WITH ROMESCO SAUCE

ROASTING PEPPERS

Roasting bell peppers (capsicums) and chile peppers loosens their skins to allow peeling and imparts a smoky flavor. To roast peppers, using tongs or a large fork, hold them over the flame or set them directly on the grate of a gas burner. Turn as needed until blistered and charred black on all sides, 10–15 minutes. Or, place the peppers under a preheated broiler (griller) as close as possible to the heating element, turning to char them on all sides. Transfer the peppers to a paper bag, close loosely, and let stand until cool, 15–30 minutes. Peel or rub away the charred skin.

To make the romesco sauce, heat the olive oil in a heavy frying pan over medium-high heat. Add the garlic and sauté until fragrant, about 30 seconds. Add the bell peppers, tomatoes, almonds, and cayenne. Simmer to blend the flavors, about 5 minutes. Transfer to a food processor or blender and add the vinegar, tomato paste, ½ teaspoon kosher salt, and ¼ teaspoon black pepper. Pulse to purée until almost smooth. Set aside. Rewarm to serve.

To make the tortilla, heat 2 tablespoons of the olive oil in a large, ovenproof frying pan over medium-high heat. Add the sliced onion and sauté until translucent, about 5 minutes. Add the potatoes, ½ teaspoon kosher salt, and ¼ teaspoon black pepper and stir to blend. Stir in ¼ cup (2 fl oz/60 ml) water. Cover, reduce the heat to medium-low, and cook, stirring occasionally, until the potatoes are tender, about 20 minutes. Uncover and simmer until any excess liquid evaporates, about 2 minutes. Transfer to a bowl and let cool, about 30 minutes. Wipe out the pan and set aside.

In a large bowl, beat the eggs, chopped onion, ½ teaspoon kosher salt, and ¼ teaspoon black pepper to blend. Add to the potatoes and stir to mix well.

Preheat the broiler (grill). Spray the reserved pan with nonstick vegetable-oil cooking spray. Add the remaining 1 tablespoon oil and heat over medium-high heat for 1 minute. Add the potato mixture, spreading evenly. Cook, uncovered, shaking the pan occasionally and loosening the sides with a spatula, until the sides are golden brown, about 8 minutes. Place the pan under the broiler 4–5 inches (10–13 cm) from the heat source. Broil (grill) until the top is set and begins to brown, about 4 minutes. Slide the tortilla onto a plate. Invert a platter over the top and invert the platter and plate together. Lift off the plate. Serve warm or at room temperature with the warm sauce.

MAKES 6 SERVINGS

FOR THE ROMESCO SAUCE:

¼ cup (2 fl oz/60 ml) olive oil

2 large cloves garlic, chopped

2 large red bell peppers (capsicums), roasted *(far left)*, peeled, seeded, and chopped

⅓ cup (2 oz/60 g) drained diced canned tomatoes

2 tablespoons sliced (flaked) almonds, toasted (page 115)

⅛ teaspoon cayenne pepper

4 teaspoons sherry vinegar

1 tablespoon tomato paste

Kosher salt and freshly ground black pepper

FOR THE TORTILLA:

3 tablespoons olive oil

3 cups (11 oz/345 g) thinly sliced yellow onion, plus ⅓ cup (2 oz/60 g) finely chopped

3 russet potatoes, about 1½ lb (750 g) total weight, peeled and cut into rounds ⅛ inch (3 mm) thick

Kosher salt and freshly ground black pepper

6 large eggs

Nonstick vegetable-oil cooking spray

POTATO AND ONION PISSALADIÈRE

**Kosher salt and coarsely
ground pepper**

**2 small russet potatoes,
about ¾ lb (375 g) total
weight, scrubbed**

**¼ cup (2 fl oz/60 ml)
olive oil**

**2 lb (1 kg) yellow onions,
halved lengthwise and
thinly sliced**

**2 teaspoons minced fresh
thyme**

**1 recipe Pastry Dough,
chilled (page 110)**

**6 oz (180 g) fresh goat
cheese, crumbled, about
1½ cups**

**12 Kalamata olives, pitted
and halved**

**8 anchovy fillets, halved
crosswise**

In a large pot of salted boiling water, boil the unpeeled whole potatoes until tender when pierced with a small knife, about 25 minutes. Transfer to a colander to drain. When cool, peel and thinly slice the potatoes. Set aside.

In a large, heavy frying pan, heat the olive oil over medium-high heat. Add the onions and sauté, stirring frequently, until beginning to brown, about 18 minutes. Sprinkle the onions with ½ teaspoon kosher salt and ¼ teaspoon pepper. Cover the pan and cook, stirring often, until the onions are deep golden, about 12 minutes longer. Remove from the heat and stir in 1½ teaspoons of the thyme. Let cool completely.

Position a rack in the bottom third of the oven and preheat the oven to 400°F (200°C).

On a lightly floured surface, roll out the dough into a 13-inch (33-cm) round. Transfer the round to a rimless baking sheet (not insulated) or a metal pizza pan. Fold in ½ inch (12 mm) of the dough edge. Then stand up and crimp the double edge, forming an 11-inch (28-cm) round with a high-standing rim. Sprinkle 1 cup (4 oz/120 g) of the cheese evenly over the dough. Top with the potato slices in a single layer. Sprinkle the potatoes lightly with pepper. Spread the onions evenly over the potatoes. Arrange the olive halves and anchovy pieces over the onions, spacing them evenly apart.

Bake the pissaladière until the crust is brown on the edges and the bottom, about 25 minutes. Sprinkle with the remaining ½ cup (2 oz/60 g) cheese and the remaining ½ teaspoon thyme. Let cool for at least 15 minutes. Serve warm or at room temperature.

MAKES 4 SERVINGS

PITTING OLIVES

Olives are a traditional part of any pissaladière, a pizzalike onion tart that is a specialty of Nice on the French Riviera. To remove the pits of olives, use a cherry pitter. If you don't own a pitter, set the olive on a work surface. Place a flat side of the blade of a large knife on the olive. Press on the blade until you feel the olive flesh come away from the pit. Then, simply pull out the pit.

POTATO SALADS

No cookbook on potatoes would be complete without a classic recipe for potato salad. This familiar favorite turns up at picnics and delis everywhere. Happily, tastes have evolved, and new forms of this old-fashioned standby are finding an appreciative audience. Contemporary additions such as olives, blue cheese, and saffron dress up the potato salads in this chapter with style.

PICNIC POTATO SALAD

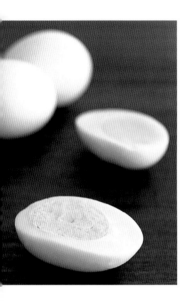

HARD-BOILED EGGS

It's easy to overcook hard-boiled eggs, giving their yolks an unsightly greenish tinge and a dry texture. The following method ensures good results: Bring a large saucepan of water to a boil over medium heat. When the water begins to boil, add the eggs and cook for 9 minutes. Lift out the eggs and place in a bowl of ice water until cool. When cool, peel the eggs.

In a small bowl, combine the red onion, white wine vinegar, dill, basil, and tarragon. In another small bowl, combine the mayonnaise, yogurt, and dry mustard and stir to blend. Set aside.

Pour water to a depth of 1 inch (2.5 cm) into a large pot and bring to a boil. Put the potatoes into a collapsible steamer basket and set the basket over the boiling water. (The water should not touch the bottom of the steamer basket.) Cover and steam until the potatoes are tender when pierced with a small knife, about 10 minutes. Transfer the potatoes to a large bowl and gently stir in the onion mixture. Let cool to lukewarm, stirring occasionally, about 15 minutes. Add the celery and coarsely chopped eggs to the potatoes, then add the mayonnaise mixture. Toss gently to combine. Season the salad with kosher salt and pepper to taste. Transfer to a serving bowl.

In a small bowl, mix the finely chopped egg and the celery leaves. Sprinkle around the edge of the salad as garnish. Serve immediately or let stand for up to 1 hour at room temperature before serving.

Make-Ahead Tip: This salad can be prepared up to 8 hours in advance, covered, and refrigerated. Bring to room temperature before serving.

Variation Tip: You can easily turn this side dish into a quick main course by adding diced ham, roast chicken, or cooked shrimp.

MAKES 6 SERVINGS

⅔ cup (3 oz/90 g) finely chopped red onion

2 tablespoons white wine vinegar

1 tablespoon minced fresh dill

1 tablespoon minced fresh basil

1 tablespoon minced fresh tarragon

½ cup (4 fl oz/125 ml) mayonnaise

¼ cup (2 oz/60 g) plain yogurt or sour cream or ¼ cup (2 fl oz/60 ml) buttermilk

½ teaspoon dry mustard

10–12 small White Rose potatoes, about 2½ lb (1.25 kg) total weight, peeled, quartered lengthwise, and each quarter halved crosswise

3 large celery stalks, finely diced

6 hard-boiled large eggs *(far left),* 5 coarsely chopped and 1 finely chopped

Kosher salt and freshly ground pepper

¼ cup (⅓ oz/10 g) finely chopped dark green celery leaves

GERMAN POTATO SALAD

Kosher salt and freshly ground pepper

12–14 very small red potatoes, about 1½ lb (750 g) total weight, scrubbed

4 slices bacon, preferably thick sliced, coarsely chopped

Olive oil as needed

½ yellow onion, halved lengthwise and thinly sliced crosswise

1 large celery stalk, thinly sliced

2 tablespoons white wine vinegar

2 teaspoons minced fresh marjoram, plus sprigs for garnish

½ teaspoon dry mustard

½ cup (4 fl oz/125 ml) beef stock (page 111) or canned beef broth

In a large pot of salted boiling water, cook the unpeeled whole potatoes until tender when pierced with a small knife, about 20 minutes. Drain well and return to the pot. Let cool for 10 minutes, then halve or quarter.

In a large, heavy frying pan, cook the bacon over medium-high heat until brown and crisp, about 6 minutes. Using a slotted spoon, transfer to paper towels to drain. Pour the drippings from the pan into a small dish.

Return 3 tablespoons of the drippings to the frying pan (if necessary, add enough olive oil to make 3 tablespoons). Add the onion and celery and sauté over medium heat until just beginning to soften, about 3 minutes. Whisk in the vinegar, minced marjoram, ¾ teaspoon kosher salt, ¼ teaspoon pepper, and dry mustard. Add the stock, potatoes, and bacon. Cook, tossing gently, until the dressing thickens and coats the potatoes, about 1 minute. Transfer the salad to a serving bowl. Garnish with the marjoram sprigs and serve warm.

MAKES 4 SERVINGS

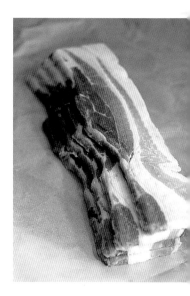

BACON

Bits of bacon and bacon fat are essential ingredients in a classic German potato salad. Look for bacon that has been smoked over apple wood, which gives it a sweet flavor. Purchase thick-sliced bacon for a more intense smoky taste. Many gourmet food stores and catalogs now feature artisanal bacon from farms where the pork is cured with flavors like maple, garlic, red pepper, and herbs and spices.

POTATOES AND GREEN BEANS WITH CUCUMBER AND YOGURT DRESSING

To make the dressing, in a bowl, whisk together the yogurt, mayonnaise, dill, oregano, ¾ teaspoon kosher salt, and ½ teaspoon pepper. Stir in the cucumber. Set aside.

Pour water to a depth of 1 inch (2.5 cm) into a large pot and bring to a boil. Put the potatoes into a collapsible steamer basket and set the basket over the boiling water. (The water should not touch the bottom of the steamer basket.) Cover and steam until the potatoes are tender when pierced with a small knife, about 14 minutes. Transfer the potatoes to a large bowl. Let cool for 5 minutes, then sprinkle lightly with kosher salt and pepper.

In the same steamer, cook the green beans until just tender-crisp, about 5 minutes. Transfer the green beans to the bowl with the potatoes. Sprinkle to taste with kosher salt and pepper and let cool to lukewarm, about 20 minutes.

Mix the vinegar into the cucumber-yogurt dressing. Stir enough of the dressing into the salad to coat generously. Serve at once.

Make-Ahead Tip: The cucumber-yogurt dressing may be prepared 1 day in advance. Cover and refrigerate.

MAKES 6 SERVINGS

CUCUMBERS

Cucumbers are an important element of tzatziki, the tangy Greek yogurt sauce that inspired the dressing for this salad. Use slender, dark green English cucumbers, also called hothouse or hydroponic cucumbers. They have thin peels and fewer and softer seeds than other varieties. A seeded cucumber will exude less liquid and won't water down the dressing. To seed, split the cucumber in half lengthwise and scoop out the seeds and surrounding pulpy matter with a teaspoon or melon baller.

FOR THE DRESSING:

⅔ cup (5 oz/155 g) plain whole-milk yogurt

⅓ cup (3 fl oz/80 ml) mayonnaise

¼ cup (⅓ oz/10 g) coarsely chopped fresh dill

½ teaspoon dried oregano

Kosher salt and freshly ground pepper

¾ cup peeled, seeded, and finely diced English (hothouse) cucumber

5 Yukon gold potatoes, about 1¾ lb (875 g) total weight, peeled, halved lengthwise, and cut crosswise into slices ⅓ inch (9 mm) thick

Kosher salt and freshly ground pepper

½ lb (250 g) green beans, trimmed and cut into 2-inch (5-cm) pieces

1½ teaspoons white wine vinegar

POTATO SALAD WITH ARTICHOKES, FETA CHEESE, AND OLIVE RELISH

FOR THE OLIVE RELISH:

5 tablespoons (3 fl oz/ 80 ml) olive oil

2 ½ tablespoons white wine vinegar

1 large clove garlic, minced

1 ½ teaspoons dried oregano

Freshly ground pepper

12 large cracked green Greek or Sicilian olives, pitted and chopped (about ⅔ cup/3½ oz/105 g)

½ cup (2½ oz/75 g) chopped fennel bulb

3 large green (spring) onions, including pale and dark green parts, chopped (about ¾ cup/2½ oz/75 g)

Kosher salt and freshly ground pepper

10 small White Rose potatoes, about 2¼ lb (1.25 g) total weight, scrubbed

1 package (8 oz/250 g) frozen artichoke hearts, thawed, patted dry, and halved lengthwise

5 oz (155 g) feta cheese, coarsely crumbled (about 1¼ cups)

To make the olive relish, combine the olive oil, white wine vinegar, garlic, oregano, and ¼ teaspoon pepper in a bowl. Whisk to blend. Stir in the olives, fennel, and two-thirds of the green onions.

In a large pot of salted boiling water, cook the unpeeled whole potatoes until tender when pierced with a small knife, about 25 minutes. Drain and let stand until cool to the touch, about 20 minutes. Peel the potatoes, cut in half lengthwise, and then crosswise into slices ⅓ inch (9 mm) thick. Transfer the potatoes to a large bowl. Sprinkle with kosher salt and pepper to taste. Add the artichokes and olive relish. Toss to blend. Stir in 1 cup (4 oz/125 g) of the feta cheese. Transfer the salad to a serving bowl.

In a small bowl, combine the remaining green onions with the remaining feta cheese. Stir to blend. Sprinkle over the salad.

Make-Ahead Tip: The olive relish can be made up to 1 day in advance. Cover and refrigerate, stirring occasionally.

MAKES 4–6 SERVINGS

FETA CHEESE

Feta, cured in brine, is a sharp, tangy cheese with a pleasantly salty flavor that is made from sheep's or sometimes goat's or cow's milk. Greece is the country best known for feta, but it is produced in other European countries as well, including Bulgaria, France, and Italy. Be aware that different brands vary in their saltiness. French feta is delicious and not too salty.

POTATO SALAD WITH RED PEPPERS, CAPERS, AND SAFFRON DRESSING

To make the dressing, combine the minced chiles, capers and caper juice, vinegar, ½ teaspoon kosher salt, ¼ teaspoon pepper, and saffron in a bowl. Whisk in the olive oil. Add the onion and toss to blend well. Let stand for at least 2 hours or up to 4 hours, stirring occasionally.

Stir the bell pepper into the dressing. In a large pot of salted boiling water, cook the unpeeled whole potatoes until tender when pierced with a small knife, about 20 minutes. Drain and let cool to the touch, about 15 minutes. Cut the potatoes into quarters and transfer to a large bowl. Add the dressing and toss to coat. Season with kosher salt and pepper to taste. Transfer to a serving bowl and garnish with chile halves, if desired.

MAKES 6 SERVINGS

SEEDING AND DEVEINING CHILES

To reduce a chile's heat, cut out the membranes, or veins, and discard the seeds. The membranes are where the capsaicin, the hot element of a chile, is primarily concentrated. Consider wearing disposable latex or plastic gloves when working with hot chiles, such as jalapeños, to avoid irritating your skin. Avoid touching sensitive areas such as your eyes or mouth. When finished, wash your hands, the cutting board, and the knife with hot, soapy water.

FOR THE SAFFRON DRESSING:

1½ large red jalapeño chiles, seeded and deveined *(far left),* then minced

1½ tablespoons drained capers, plus 1½ teaspoons caper juice

2 tablespoons white wine vinegar

Kosher salt and freshly ground pepper

¼ teaspoon saffron threads

¼ cup (2 fl oz/60 ml) olive oil

1 large red onion, halved lengthwise and cut cross-wise into paper-thin slices (about 2 cups/7 oz/220 g)

1 large red bell pepper (capsicum), seeded, deveined, and cut into matchsticks

Kosher salt and freshly ground pepper

12 small red potatoes, about 2 lb (1 kg) total weight, scrubbed

3 red jalapeño chiles, halved lengthwise (optional)

84

FRENCH COUNTRY POTATO SALAD

FOR THE DRESSING:

3 tablespoons white wine vinegar

2 tablespoons Dijon mustard

1 tablespoon minced fresh rosemary

3 cloves garlic, minced

⅛ teaspoon ground allspice

6 tablespoons (3 fl oz/ 90 ml) olive oil

Kosher salt and freshly ground pepper

12 small red potatoes, about 2 lb (1 kg) total weight, scrubbed

1 large leek, including pale green parts, halved length-wise and well rinsed (page 18), then chopped

½ lb (250 g) fully cooked smoked sausage such as kielbasa, cut into rounds ¼ inch (6 mm) thick

2 oz (60 g) Roquefort cheese, coarsely crumbled (about ½ cup)

Kosher salt and freshly ground pepper

Fresh rosemary sprigs for garnish

To make the dressing, whisk together the white wine vinegar, Dijon mustard, rosemary, garlic, and allspice in a small bowl. Gradually whisk in the olive oil. Season to taste with kosher salt and pepper.

In a large pot of salted boiling water, cook the unpeeled whole potatoes until tender when pierced with a small knife, about 20 minutes. Drain and let stand until cool to the touch, about 15 minutes. Peel the potatoes and cut them into rounds ⅓ inch (9 mm) thick.

Put the potatoes in a large bowl and add ¼ cup (2 fl oz/60 ml) of the dressing. Toss gently to coat, separating the potato slices. Stir in the leek, then the sausage and remaining dressing. Stir in the cheese and season to taste with kosher salt and pepper. Transfer to a serving bowl and garnish with rosemary sprigs.

MAKES 6 SERVINGS

BLUE CHEESE

Blue cheeses are inoculated with the spores of special molds to develop a fine network of blue veins. Roquefort, the premier sheep's milk blue cheese from France, has a strong, pungent flavor that adds a decidedly French accent to any dish, making it a natural choice for this recipe. Other blue cheeses you could also use are English Stilton, Danish Blue, Italian Gorgonzola, or Maytag Blue from the American Midwest.

BREAKFAST POTATOES

Filling and packed with nutrition, potatoes are exactly what we need in the morning. They can be sweet and spread with honey butter in pancakes or spiced up with chiles in a frittata. Many of the recipes that follow are perfect for entertaining and may just make breakfast your favorite meal of the day.

HASH BROWNS

In a large pot of salted boiling water, cook the unpeeled whole potatoes until tender when pierced with a small knife, about 25 minutes. Drain, let cool, and refrigerate until cold, at least 2 hours or up to 1 day. Peel the potatoes and shred *(left)* into a large bowl. Add 1 teaspoon kosher salt and ½ teaspoon pepper. Toss to blend.

In a heavy, 12-inch (30-cm) nonstick frying pan, melt 3 tablespoons of the butter with the oil over high heat. Add the potatoes, reduce the heat to medium, and cook for 5 minutes, tossing to coat the potatoes evenly with the butter. Using a heatproof, plastic spatula, press the potatoes lightly to compact into a 9-inch (23-cm) round. Continue to cook until beginning to brown on the bottom, about 10 minutes. Using the spatula, turn the potatoes over in sections. Press again to flatten to an even thickness. Dot with the remaining 1 tablespoon butter. Continue to cook, pressing the edges of the round in neatly and shaking the pan occasionally to prevent sticking, about 12 minutes.

Slide the potato round out onto a large plate. Invert another large plate on top and, holding the plates together, invert them. Slide the potato round back into the pan. Cook over medium heat until the bottom is brown and crusty, about 10 minutes longer. Slide the potato cake out onto a platter. Sprinkle with the parsley, if desired. Cut into wedges and serve hot.

MAKES 4 SERVINGS

Kosher salt and freshly ground pepper

6 small White Rose potatoes or medium red potatoes, about 1½ lb (750 g) total weight, scrubbed

4 tablespoons (2 oz/60 g) unsalted butter

1 tablespoon vegetable oil

2–3 tablespoons minced fresh flat-leaf (Italian) parsley (optional)

HOME FRIES WITH RED, WHITE, AND GREEN ONIONS

Kosher salt and freshly ground pepper

3 large Yukon gold potatoes, about 1½ lb (750 g) total weight, scrubbed

3 tablespoons unsalted butter

1 tablespoon olive oil

1 cup (4½ oz/140 g) diced red onion

1 cup (4½ oz/140 g) diced white onion

4 green (spring) onions, including pale and dark green parts, chopped (about 1 cup/3 oz/90 g)

In a large pot of salted boiling water, cook the unpeeled whole potatoes until tender when pierced with a small knife, about 35 minutes. Drain the potatoes, let them cool, and refrigerate them until cold, at least 2 hours or up to 1 day. Peel the potatoes and cut into ½-inch (12-mm) cubes.

In a large, heavy nonstick frying pan, melt 2 tablespoons of the butter with the oil over medium-high heat. Add the potatoes, red onion, and white onion and toss to coat. Sauté, tossing every 3 or 4 minutes, until the potatoes are light brown and the onions are just beginning to brown, about 15 minutes total. Sprinkle with 1 teaspoon kosher salt and ½ teaspoon pepper. Toss to blend. Cook until the potatoes and onions are golden brown, about 5 minutes longer. Add the green onions and remaining 1 table-spoon butter. Toss until the butter melts and the green onions just wilt, about 1 minute. Transfer the home fries to a bowl and serve.

MAKES 4 SERVINGS

DICING ONIONS

To dice an onion, trim the stem end and halve the onion length-wise. Peel the halves. Place one half, flat side down, on a cutting board. Starting at the stem end, make a series of parallel horizontal cuts ¼–½ inch (6–12 mm) apart. Do not cut all the way through the root end. Turn the knife so it is perpendicular to the first series of cuts and so the tip is pointed toward the root end and make a similar series of vertical cuts, again leaving the root end intact. To dice, slice across both series of cuts.

SWEET POTATO PANCAKES
WITH ORANGE-HONEY BUTTER

To make the orange-honey butter, combine the butter, honey, orange juice concentrate, and orange zest in a bowl. Beat with an electric mixer until blended.

To make the pancakes, peel the yam and cut crosswise into slices ½ inch (12 mm) thick. Pour water to a depth of 1 inch (2.5 cm) into a saucepan and bring to a boil. Put the yam slices into a collapsible steamer basket and set the basket over the boiling water. (The water should not touch the bottom of the steamer basket.) Cover and steam until just tender when pierced with a small knife, about 8 minutes. Transfer the slices to a plate and refrigerate until cold and firm, at least 1 hour.

Place a baking sheet in the oven and preheat to 225°F (110°C). Using the large shredding holes of a box grater-shredder, shred the yam into a bowl. In a large bowl, whisk together the flour, sugar, baking powder, kosher salt, and ginger. Add the buttermilk, eggs, and the 1 tablespoon melted butter. Whisk just until blended (some lumps will remain). Stir in 1 cup (6 oz/185 g) of the yam. (Reserve the remaining yam for another use.)

Heat a large, nonstick frying pan over medium-low heat. Brush the pan with melted butter. Ladle a scant ¼ cup (2 fl oz/60 ml) of the batter into the pan for each pancake, 1–2 inches (2.5–5 cm) apart. Cook the pancakes until they are golden brown on the bottom and bubbles have formed but have not yet broken on the top, about 3 minutes. Flip the pancakes and cook until golden brown on the second side, about 3 minutes longer. Transfer the pancakes to the baking sheet in the oven to keep warm. Repeat with the remaining batter. Serve the pancakes topped with a small scoop of the orange-honey butter and garnish with orange segments.

MAKES 4 SERVINGS

SEGMENTING CITRUS FRUIT

To segment an orange or other citrus fruit, cut a slice off the top and bottom of the fruit down to the flesh, then stand it upright. Following the contour of the fruit, slice off the peel and white pith in thick strips, to reveal the flesh. Holding the fruit over a bowl, cut on either side of each membrane to release the segments into the bowl.

You can also use orange segments in fruit salad or to garnish molded desserts such as panna cotta or flan.

FOR THE ORANGE-HONEY BUTTER:

½ cup (4 oz/125 g) unsalted butter, at room temperature

½ cup (6 oz/185 g) honey

¼ cup (2 fl oz/60 ml) thawed frozen orange juice concentrate

1½ teaspoons grated orange zest

FOR THE PANCAKES:

1 small yam (orange-fleshed sweet potato), about ½ lb (250 g)

1⅓ cups (7 oz/220 g) all-purpose (plain) flour

3 tablespoons sugar

2 teaspoons baking powder

¾ teaspoon kosher salt

¼ teaspoon ground ginger

1 cup (8 fl oz/250 ml) buttermilk

2 large eggs, beaten

1 tablespoon unsalted butter, melted, plus ⅓–½ cup (3–4 oz/90–125 g) unsalted butter, melted, for brushing

2 oranges, segmented (far left)

94

SWEET POTATO AND BACON FRITTERS

½ lb (250 g) bacon, coarsely chopped

1 large yam (orange-fleshed sweet potato), 12–14 oz (375–440 g), scrubbed and patted dry

½ cup (4 fl oz/125 ml) buttermilk, or more as needed

1 large egg, beaten

2 cups (10 oz/315 g) all-purpose (plain) flour

¼ cup (2 oz/60 g) sugar

3 tablespoons chilled unsalted butter, cut into pieces

1 tablespoon baking powder

¾ teaspoon kosher salt

¼ teaspoon freshly grated nutmeg

¼ teaspoon ground allspice

Vegetable oil for deep-frying

Pure maple syrup for serving

Preheat the oven to 400°F (200°C). In a large, heavy skillet, cook the bacon over medium-high heat until brown and crisp, about 5 minutes. Using a slotted spoon, transfer to paper towels to drain.

Prick the yam several times with a fork, put directly on an oven rack, and bake until tender when pierced with a knife, about 55 minutes. Alternatively, cook the yam in the microwave on high heat until tender, about 6 minutes on each side. Remove the yam and reduce the oven heat to 275°F (135°C).

Cut the yam open and let cool for 5 minutes. Spoon the flesh into a bowl and mash with a potato masher. Measure out ½ cup (4 oz/125 g) of the mashed yam and place it in a large bowl. (Reserve any remaining yam for another use.) Whisk in the buttermilk and egg.

Blend the flour, sugar, butter, baking powder, kosher salt, nutmeg, and allspice in a food processor until a fine meal forms. Add the flour mixture to the yam mixture and stir until a soft dough forms, adding more buttermilk, 1 tablespoon at a time, if the dough is dry. Add the bacon and stir just until distributed. Cover the bowl with a kitchen towel and let stand for 10 minutes.

Line a baking sheet with paper towels. Pour vegetable oil to a depth of 1½ inches (4 cm) into a Dutch oven with a deep-frying thermometer attached to the side. Heat the oil over medium heat until it registers 350°F (180°C). Drop level tablespoonfuls of the dough, 5 or 6 at a time, into the oil and fry, turning occasionally, until cooked through and brown, about 3 minutes. Using a slotted spoon, transfer the fritters to the baking sheet. Place in the oven to keep warm. Repeat with the remaining batter, letting the oil return to 350°F between each batch and using a slotted spoon to remove any bits. Serve the fritters hot with maple syrup.

MAKES 6 SERVINGS

MAPLE SYRUP

With a flavor reminiscent of vanilla and caramel, pure maple syrup is made from the sap of the sugar maple tree. In early spring, throughout Canada and the northern United States, clear, fresh sap is tapped from trees and boiled down to make a rich, amber syrup. Maple syrup is graded according to its quality and color. The lighter the color, the more mild the syrup and the higher the grade. Use lighter syrups on pancakes and fritters, reserving darker syrups for baking. Avoid caramel-colored, maple-flavored corn syrup, also called pancake syrup; it has no relation to the real thing.

FRENCH-QUARTER POTATOES

ANDOUILLE SAUSAGE
Heavily smoked and spicy, andouille sausage is a New Orleans staple and is used readily in Cajun recipes such as gumbo. Made from pork, it is generously seasoned with cayenne pepper and dried crushed red pepper. You could also use other fully cooked smoked sausages in this recipe, such as Polish kielbasa, hot links, or Portuguese linguiça flavored with garlic and paprika.

In a small bowl, stir together the Creole mustard, Worcestershire sauce, cayenne, and allspice. Set aside.

In a large, heavy nonstick frying pan, heat the olive oil over medium heat. Add the potatoes, bay leaves, and a scant ¼ teaspoon black pepper. Stir to coat. Cover and cook, stirring occasionally, until the potatoes are tender and beginning to brown, about 15 minutes. Add the garlic and stir until fragrant, about 30 seconds. Add the red onion and bell pepper. Raise the heat to medium-high and sauté, uncovered, until tender, about 6 minutes. Add the sausage and stir until heated through, about 2 minutes. Add the mustard mixture and toss for 1 minute to coat.

Remove and discard the bay leaves. Transfer the potato mixture to a serving bowl. Sprinkle generously with the green onions and serve at once.

Note: Creole mustard, made with brown mustard seeds that have been steeped in vinegar, has a touch of horseradish and a special kick. You can find Creole mustard in specialty-food stores and well-stocked supermarkets.

Serving Tip: Try serving these potatoes alongside scrambled eggs.

MAKES 4 SERVINGS

2 tablespoons Creole mustard (see Note)

1 tablespoon Worcestershire sauce

⅛ teaspoon cayenne pepper

⅛ teaspoon ground allspice

3 tablespoons olive oil

5 small White Rose potatoes, about 1¼ lb (625 g) total weight, peeled and cut into ½-inch (12-mm) cubes

4 bay leaves, preferably Turkish (page 10)

Freshly ground black pepper

6 large cloves garlic, minced

1½ cups (7½ oz/235 g) chopped red onion

1½ cups (7½ oz/235 g) chopped green bell pepper (capsicum)

4 andouille sausage links, about ¾ lb (375 g) total weight, quartered length-wise and then cut crosswise into ½-inch (12-mm) dice

2 green (spring) onions, including pale and dark green parts, chopped

CORNED BEEF HASH WITH POACHED EGGS

Kosher salt and freshly
ground pepper

6 red potatoes, about
1½ lb (750 g) total weight,
scrubbed

6 tablespoons (½ oz/15 g)
minced fresh flat-leaf
(Italian) parsley

3 tablespoons Dijon
mustard

¾ cup (3½ oz/105 g) finely
chopped red onion

¾ lb (375 g) thick-sliced
cooked corned beef
(far right), finely diced

3 tablespoons unsalted
butter

1 tablespoon cider vinegar

4 large eggs

In a large saucepan of salted boiling water, cook the unpeeled whole potatoes until just tender when pierced with a small knife, about 20 minutes. Drain, let cool, and peel. Put 2 potatoes in a large bowl and mash well with a fork. Stir in 4 tablespoons (⅓ oz/10 g) of the parsley, the mustard, and ¼ teaspoon pepper, then stir in the onion. Finely dice the remaining 4 potatoes. Mix the diced potatoes and corned beef into the mashed potato mixture.

In a large, heavy 12-inch (30-cm) nonstick frying pan, melt the butter over high heat. Add the potato mixture to the pan, pressing with a heatproof plastic spatula to compact. Cover, reduce the heat to medium, and cook until the bottom is brown, about 12 minutes. Using the spatula, turn the mixture over in sections. Press again to compact. Cover and cook until the second side is brown, about 10 minutes longer.

Meanwhile, poach the eggs. In a large frying pan, pour in water to a depth of 2 inches (5 cm), add the vinegar, and bring to a simmer over medium-high heat. Reduce the heat so the water is just under a boil. Break an egg into a saucer. While swirling the water in the pan, gently slip the egg into the swirl to prevent the whites from spreading. Quickly repeat with the remaining eggs. Poach until the whites are set and the yolks are glazed but still soft, 3–4 minutes.

Meanwhile, divide the hash into 4 equal portions and transfer to individual plates. Using a slotted spoon, transfer a poached egg to the top of each portion. Sprinkle with the remaining 2 tablespoons parsley and serve.

Note: Poached eggs are not fully cooked. For more information, see page 113.

MAKES 4 SERVINGS

CORNED BEEF

Purplish red and mildly spicy, corned beef is beef brisket or round that has been cured for about 1 month in a brine made from large crystals, or corns, of salt, sugar, and other seasonings. When slowly simmered in water, the beef develops a moist, tender texture. Buy corned beef from a Jewish delicatessen or the deli section in your market so that you can ask for slices ⅓ inch (9 mm) thick.

POTATO FRITTATA WITH AVOCADO AND THREE-CHILE SALSA

SEEDING TOMATOES

Before seeding and chopping tomatoes, wash and dry them. Using a serrated knife, cut each tomato in half crosswise. Holding each half in turn over a sink, lightly squeeze and shake it to dislodge the seeds. Use your finger if needed to help ease the seeds out of each half. Cut out the stem end and chop as directed.

In a bowl, combine the red onion and the poblano, Anaheim, and jalapeño chiles. Toss to mix. Transfer ½ cup (2½ oz/75 g) of the chile mixture to another bowl and stir in the tomatoes, avocado, cilantro, and lime juice. Toss together to make the salsa. Season to taste with kosher salt. Cover and refrigerate.

Spray a heavy nonstick 10-inch (25-cm) frying pan with nonstick vegetable-oil cooking spray. Add 1 tablespoon of the olive oil and heat over medium heat. Add the remaining chile mixture to the pan and sauté until the chiles just begin to soften, about 7 minutes. Transfer to a large bowl. Add 2 more tablespoons of the olive oil to same pan. Add the potatoes and ¼ teaspoon kosher salt and stir to blend. Cover, reduce the heat to medium-low, and cook, stirring occasionally, until the potatoes are tender, about 10 minutes (some potatoes may brown). Add the potatoes to the bowl with the chile mixture and let cool to lukewarm.

In a small bowl, beat the eggs with ½ teaspoon kosher salt to blend. Stir the eggs into the potato mixture. Spray the same frying pan lightly with nonstick cooking spray. Add the remaining 1 tablespoon olive oil and heat over medium-high heat. Add the egg-potato mixture to the pan. Cook, running a heatproof plastic spatula around the edge of the pan occasionally to loosen the frittata, until the sides are set, about 6 minutes. Cover and cook until the center of the frittata is set, about 9 minutes longer. Run the spatula around the edge and under the center of the frittata to loosen. Slide the frittata onto a plate and invert a serving platter on top. Holding the plate and platter together, invert them and lift off the plate. Garnish with lime wedges, if desired. Cut the frittata into wedges and serve with the salsa.

MAKES 4 SERVINGS

1 cup (5 oz/155 g) chopped red onion

⅓ cup (1½ oz/45 g) chopped seeded poblano chile

⅓ cup (1½ oz/45 g) chopped seeded Anaheim chile

1 tablespoon minced jalapeño chile with seeds

2 large plum (Roma) tomatoes, seeded and chopped (far left)

1 avocado, pitted, peeled, and diced

3 tablespoons chopped fresh cilantro (fresh coriander)

4 teaspoons fresh lime juice

Kosher salt

Nonstick vegetable-oil cooking spray

4 tablespoons (2 fl oz/60 ml) olive oil

3 red potatoes, about ¾ lb (375 g) total weight, scrubbed, patted dry, halved, and cut crosswise into slices ⅛ inch (3 mm) thick

6 large eggs

Lime wedges for garnish (optional)

POTATO BASICS

Like a blank canvas, potatoes are a promising starting point. They can be prepared by most cooking methods and blended with countless ingredients to create delicious results. Their versatility and reliability make them a good choice for nearly any menu, whether casual or celebratory. Today, such staples as corn, beans, and greens are being rediscovered and given new culinary status by appreciative chefs. Potatoes deserve to be among their honored ranks.

POTATO TYPES

The starchy tubers of a plant that is part of the nightshade family, potatoes have become one of the world's most important crops. Nutritious and easy to digest, this staple vegetable is a valuable source of carbohydrates, protein, and fiber as well as vitamins such as vitamin C and minerals such as potassium and iron.

Potatoes can be divided into three basic types: starchy or mealy, waxy, and all-purpose. Starchy potatoes, such as russets, are best for baking and mashing because they cook up dry and fluffy but do not hold their shape well. Waxier potatoes, such as red potatoes, are low in starch. They are ideal for potato salads and other recipes where the tubers must hold their shape but do not need to contribute their starch to thicken a soup or sauce. All-purpose potatoes have a medium starch content and are good for both uses. Yukon golds are among the best known.

Following is a list of the potato varieties used throughout this book.

RUSSET POTATOES

Oblong, dark brown–skinned russet potatoes are mealy due to their high starch and low moisture content. When cooked, they have a fluffy, dry texture that makes them ideal for baking and for making crisp French fries with tender interiors. Use them for mashed potatoes when a fluffy texture is desired. Russets are also known as Burbank or Idaho potatoes.

RED POTATOES

Sometimes known as boiling potatoes, these smooth-skinned, firm potatoes are high in moisture and low in starch. They hold their shape very well during cooking and have a dense and moist texture. Red potatoes are one of the best choices for boiling, steaming, and roasting and for potato salads. The most widely available varieties, such as Red La Soda and Red Pontiac, are round, 2–3 inches (5–7.5 cm) in diameter, and have dusky red skins. Very small, young red potatoes are sometimes called creamers.

WHITE POTATOES

These thin-skinned potatoes are considered all-purpose because their flesh is not as dry as that of starchy baking potatoes nor as waxy as that of red potatoes. White Rose, developed in California, are long, oval potatoes with thin, cream-colored skin and relatively few, very small eyes. They are found in most markets and can be used successfully for baking, boiling, roasting, and steaming. Similarly, round whites, such as the Eastern Kennebec, Superior, and Katahdin, are all-purpose potatoes. Tiny, young white potatoes are called creamers or baby new potatoes.

YUKON GOLDS

These distinctive all-purpose boiling potatoes, with pale gold skin and flesh, have a dense texture and somewhat buttery flavor. They make sumptuous mashed potatoes and are wonderful roasted, boiled, or steamed.

NEW POTATOES

Immature, new potatoes typically fill the market bins in spring and early summer. They are usually of the round red or round white variety, although you may also find new Yellow Finns. New potatoes are low in starch. Be aware that not all small potatoes are new. A true new potato is freshly harvested and will have a thin skin and a short shelf life.

FINGERLING POTATOES

Because of their long, narrow shape, certain potato varieties are called fingerlings. Low in starch, they are good roasted, steamed, or boiled. For more information on fingerling varieties, see page 47.

CHOOSING POTATOES

Just as you'd choose other vegetables, look for potatoes that are firm, unblemished, and uniform in shape. The buds of the potato, commonly called eyes, should not have sprouted. (If you have potatoes at home that have sprouted, cut out the eyes before using.) Wrinkled skin, soft flesh, and sprouts indicate potatoes that are past their prime. If a potato has some green portions, it has been exposed to light for too long and a toxic alkaloid called solanine has developed. Don't buy these potatoes. If your stored potatoes take on a green cast, cut these portions away before using.

If you are planning to eat unpeeled potatoes, consider buying organic varieties. Organic potatoes have not been exposed to pesticides, which can concentrate in the skin. Organic potatoes can be found in dedicated produce sections at many supermarkets, at natural-foods stores, and at many open-air farmers' markets.

Most potato varieties are available year-round, but new potatoes appear only in the spring and early summer and sporadically at other times.

STORING POTATOES

When storing potatoes, select a fairly dark place at cool room temperature with good air circulation, as light causes them to turn green and bitter. If potatoes have been purchased in plastic, transfer them to a large brown paper bag or sheltered vegetable bin where they will keep well for up to 2 weeks. (Storing potatoes in plastic prevents ventilation and accelerates spoilage.) Avoid keeping potatoes in the refrigerator, where the cold temperature will convert some of the potatoes' starch to sugar, making them sweet. Do not put potatoes in the same bin with onions. Together, these vegetables produce gases that cause rapid spoilage.

Use new potatoes, which have a much shorter shelf life than other potato varieties, within 2 or 3 days of purchase.

PREPARING POTATOES

Potatoes can be cooked in just about every way imaginable: boiled, baked, steamed, roasted, deep-fried, sautéed, or simmered in soups. They can also take many forms, such as fine shreds, thick batons, big or small cubes, purée, or whole, skin and all. Following are some tips to help you prepare potatoes.

WASHING

Whether or not you plan to peel potatoes, always wash them under cold running water, preferably using a clean sponge. Unlike a stiff-bristled brush, the sponge won't tear or cut the skin when rubbing away dirt.

PEELING

The most efficient tool for peeling potatoes is a sturdy swivel-blade vegetable peeler with a heavy, nonslip or rubber handle and a small pointed scoop at the tip end for removing eyes or sprouts.

Since potatoes discolor rather quickly once they are peeled, it is best to prepare other parts of the recipe first, then peel the potatoes

just before using them. If necessary, keep peeled potatoes in a bowl of cold water to cover for a short period of time. If you keep them in water for longer than 30 minutes they will begin to lose nutrients in the water.

STEAMING

A collapsible stainless-steel steamer basket, or rack, with a center handle is perfect for steaming potatoes. The sides of these baskets consist of overlapping panels that open flat like the petals of a flower. The panels should rest loosely against the sides of the pot in order to prevent the potatoes from falling into the water. The handle in the center of the basket allows the cooked potatoes to be lifted easily out of the pot. The water level in the pot should be at least 1 inch (2.5 cm) deep but ½ inch (12 mm) lower than the bottom of the basket so the water doesn't boil up into the potatoes.

A quick way to steam potatoes is to cut them into rounds ¼ inch (6 mm) thick or into ½-inch (12-mm) dice. Steaming potato pieces in this way preserves texture, flavor, and nutrients that can be lost when the pieces are boiled. Bring the water to a boil before adding the potatoes to the basket. Cover the pot tightly and steam until a small knife meets no resistance when thrust into a potato piece. If steaming whole potatoes, which take longer, occasionally fold up one of the steamer basket panels to check the water level in the pan, and replenish with more boiling water if necessary.

BOILING

The best way to boil potatoes is whole with their skins on. This keeps them from becoming waterlogged and helps to prevent nutrients from being lost in the water. When boiling whole potatoes, make sure the potato skins are not broken so the nutrients will be better preserved.

To boil potatoes, fill a pot with water, leaving some room for the potatoes to be added. Bring the water to a boil and sprinkle in a generous amount of kosher salt, a little at a time, or the water may boil over. Add the potatoes to the pot and cook for the time indicated in the recipe before testing for doneness. Test the largest potato first, because if it is done, the smaller ones will be, too. Usually, once the skins start to split, the potatoes are cooked through.

If you are boiling peeled potatoes, be sure to cut them into small pieces, 1 inch (2.5 cm) or less. They will cook faster and spend less time in the water, where they can lose nutrients and become mushy in texture.

MASHING

Mashed potatoes can be made in a number of ways. You can start with boiled whole, unpeeled potatoes or steamed peeled potato rounds or dice. For an entire chapter of mashed potato recipes, see pages 26–37.

Shown opposite are the basic steps for making mashed potatoes using whole, unpeeled potatoes.

1 **Cooking whole potatoes:** Start with whole unpeeled potatoes and cook them in a large pot of salted boiling water until tender, 20–40 minutes, depending on the potatoes' size. When the skins begin to split, the potatoes are cooked through. (For instructions on steaming potato cubes, see above.) Drain the potatoes and empty the water from the pot. Add the butter called for in a recipe to the still-warm pot so it begins to melt.

2 **Peeling whole potatoes:** While the potatoes are still hot, use a large two-pronged fork or a pot holder to hold each potato, then peel with a paring knife. The skins should come off easily.

3 **Mashing:** Return the still-hot potatoes to the pot with the butter. The heat from the potatoes will help melt the butter. Mash the potatoes until fairly smooth.

4 **Adding milk:** Mix in the milk or cream and other ingredients. (If desired, warm the milk or cream first to help keep the potatoes from becoming cold as you finish mixing.) Adjust the texture by gradually adding more milk or cream, 1 tablespoon at a time, as needed to reach the desired consistency.

You can alter the texture of mashed potatoes depending on the mashing tool you use. A handheld masher will produce mashed potatoes with a coarse texture. It doesn't over-work the potatoes and doesn't activate their starches, which means the end result will not be gummy. A ricer uses a plunger to force the potatoes through a pattern of small holes. This action breaks them up finely to yield smooth, fluffy mashed potatoes. An electric mixer will whip potatoes to a fluffy mass. To avoid overbeating them, first mash them a little by hand with the butter to break up the biggest lumps. Then whip them to the desired consistency, adding the remaining ingredients. Do not use a food processor or you will end up with a dense, gummy texture.

If adding sautéed leeks, cabbage, spinach, yellow onions, or other substantial ingredients to mashed potatoes, first mash the potatoes with the butter and milk and then use a large spoon to stir in the additional ingredients by hand.

The leanest way to make mashed potatoes is to use vegetable or chicken stock or broth for the liquid instead of milk or cream. For real calorie savings, reserve some of the potato cooking water to use for mashing with the potatoes.

BAKING

For instructions on how to bake potatoes as well as ideas for toppings, see page 111.

ROASTING

Roasting potatoes in the dry heat of the oven will yield crisp brown crusts and tender centers. To roast, position an oven rack in the center of the oven and preheat the oven to the required temperature for at least 15 minutes. Use heavy roasting pans or baking sheets to prevent the metal from buckling and to safeguard the potatoes from getting scorched while roasting. Even if the potatoes are coated in oil, spray the baking sheet or pan with vegetable oil spray to ensure that crusty parts will not stick to the surface.

If roasting whole peeled potatoes, make sure to wipe them dry with kitchen towels or paper towels before seasoning them. The dry surface will hold any coating of herbs and spices better and will yield a better crust. Turn them with tongs rather than a fork to avoid piercing them.

If roasting potato slices, wedges, or cubes, dry them well before you season them. Turn them over with a thin flexible spatula that will keep the pieces intact and will not tear away any of the developing crust.

BASIC RECIPES

Here are four recipes referred to throughout this book.

PASTRY DOUGH

1 cup (5 oz/155 g) all-purpose (plain) flour

1 tablespoon sugar

½ teaspoon salt

6 tablespoons (3 oz/90 g) chilled unsalted butter, cut into ½-inch (12-mm) cubes

3 tablespoons ice water, plus more as needed

To make the pastry dough, combine the flour, sugar, and salt in a food processor and process for about 5 seconds. Add the butter and toss with the flour to coat. Pulse until the mixture resembles coarse meal. Add the 3 tablespoons ice water and process until the dough forms moist clumps. Alternatively, make the dough by hand: In a bowl, whisk together the flour, sugar, and salt. Add the butter and, using 2 knives or a pastry blender, cut in the butter until the mixture resembles coarse meal. Slowly add the 3 tablespoons ice water, stirring and tossing with a fork until the dough just holds together. For either method, add more ice water by teaspoonfuls if the dough is dry.

Gather the dough into a ball, flatten into a disk, wrap in plastic, and refrigerate for at least 1 hour or up to 1 day. Makes enough for one 9-inch (23-cm) tart or one 11-inch (28-cm) pissaladière.

BASIC BAKED POTATOES

**4 russet potatoes, 8–10 oz (250–315 g)
each, scrubbed and patted dry**

**4 teaspoons olive oil or melted butter
(optional)**

Position a rack in the upper third of the oven
and preheat the oven to 400°F (200°C). Pierce
the potatoes in a few places with a fork.
For a delicate crisp skin, rub each potato
with 1 teaspoon olive oil or butter. If you
are planning to use the potatoes for another
recipe or if you would like a harder, crustier
skin, omit the oil. Place the potatoes directly
on the oven rack.

Bake the potatoes until tender when pierced
with a knife, 45 minutes–1 hour.

If using the potatoes for another dish, proceed
as directed in that recipe. If serving them
immediately, use a pot holder to grasp each
potato and cut lengthwise through the top to
reach halfway through its depth. Press in the
sides to force the top open. Fill with a topping
as desired; see below. Makes 4 servings.

Suggested Toppings:

*Diced mushrooms sautéed in butter with fresh
herbs and shallots and mixed with crispy
crumbled bacon.*

*Crème fraîche (page 113) mixed with chopped
chives and prepared white cream-style
horseradish, and topped with caviar.*

*Softened butter blended with crumbled
Roquefort cheese and minced red onion.*

*Seeded diced plum (Roma) tomatoes mixed
with olive oil, chopped Kalamata olives,
chopped fresh basil, and feta cheese.*

CHICKEN STOCK

4 lb (2 kg) chicken wings, rinsed

4 qt (4 l) cold water

2 yellow onions, halved

**2 celery stalks, cut into 1-inch (2.5-cm)
pieces**

**1 large leek, white and pale green parts
only, halved lengthwise**

**1 large carrot, cut into 1-inch (2.5-cm)
pieces**

4 large flat-leaf (Italian) parsley sprigs

¼ teaspoon kosher salt

6 whole black peppercorns

3 whole cloves

Combine all the ingredients in a heavy stockpot. Bring to a boil over high heat, reduce the
heat to medium-low, and simmer, uncovered,
for 2¼ hours.

Line a large colander with a damp piece of
cheesecloth (muslin). Strain the stock through
the colander into a large bowl, pressing on
the solids with the back of a spoon. Let cool
at room temperature for 1 hour, then refrigerate, uncovered, until the fat has hardened
on top, at least 6 hours and up to 1 day. Lift
off the fat and discard. Cover and refrigerate
for up to 3 days or freeze for up to 3 months.
Makes 7 cups (56 fl oz/1.75 l).

BEEF STOCK

¼ cup (2 fl oz/60 ml) vegetable oil

**4 lb (2 kg) meaty beef neck bones, cut into
1½- to 2-inch (4- to 5-cm) pieces**

3 yellow onions, sliced

**2 large celery stalks, cut into 1-inch
(2.5-cm) pieces**

2 large plum (Roma) tomatoes, halved

3 large cloves garlic, halved

4 qt (4 l) cold water

6 fresh flat-leaf (Italian) parsley sprigs

¼ teaspoon kosher salt

12 whole black peppercorns

4 whole allspice

1 bay leaf, preferably Turkish (page 10)

In a large heavy stockpot, heat the oil over
medium-high heat. Add the bones and sauté
until deep brown, about 10 minutes. Transfer
to a bowl. Add the onions and celery to the
pot and sauté until deep brown, about 20 minutes. Add the tomatoes and garlic and stir for
1 minute. Add all the remaining ingredients
and the bones with any accumulated juices,
bring to a boil, reduce the heat to medium-
low, and simmer, uncovered, for 4 hours.

Line a large colander with a damp piece of
cheesecloth (muslin). Strain the stock through
the colander into a large bowl, pressing on
the solids with the back of a spoon. Let cool
at room temperature for 1 hour, then refrigerate, uncovered, until the fat has hardened
on top, at least 6 hours and up to 1 day. Lift
off the fat and discard. Cover and refrigerate
for up to 3 days or freeze for up to 3 months.
Makes 6 cups (48 fl oz/1.5 l).

GLOSSARY

ALLSPICE These small dark brown dried berries from the pimiento tree have a mixed-spice flavor evoking cinnamon, clove, nutmeg, ginger, and pepper. Also referred to as Jamaican pepper, allspice can be purchased ground or whole and is used in both sweet and savory dishes.

BUTTERMILK Traditionally, buttermilk is the liquid left behind when butter is churned from cream. Today, most buttermilk is a form of cultured lowfat or nonfat milk in which the sugars have turned to acids. Buttermilk adds a tangy flavor and thick, creamy texture to dressings, batters, and baked goods.

BUTTER, UNSALTED Made from churned sweet cream, most butter is 80 percent milk fat and the rest is water and milk solids. Many cooks favor unsalted butter for two reasons: First, salt in butter can add to the total amount of salt in a recipe, which can interfere with the taste of the final dish. Second, unsalted butter is likely to be fresher, since salt acts as a preservative and prolongs shelf life. If you cannot find unsalted butter, salted butter will work in most recipes, but taste and adjust other salt in the recipe as needed.

CAPERS Flower buds from a shrub native to the Mediterranean, capers are usually sold pickled in a vinegar brine. Those labeled nonpareils, from the south of France, are the smallest and considered the best.

CAYENNE PEPPER A very hot ground red pepper made from dried cayenne and other chiles, cayenne can be used sparingly in a wide variety of recipes to add heat or heighten flavor. Always begin with a small amount and add more to taste in tiny increments.

CHIVES A delicately flavored herb from the onion family, chives look like thin green tapered straws. Avoid dried chives, which have little taste. Chopped green (spring) onion tops are an acceptable substitute.

CILANTRO The bright green stems and leaves from the coriander plant, cilantro, also known as Chinese parsley, is used extensively in Mexican, Asian, Indian, Latin, and Middle Eastern cuisines.

COLANDER This bowl-shaped metal or heavy-duty plastic device is perforated with small holes. It is indispensable for draining boiled foods such as potatoes or pasta and for rinsing large quantities of fruits or vegetables. A colander lined with damp cheesecloth (muslin) can also be used for straining stock.

CORNICHONS Also called gherkins, cornichons are prepared with cucumbers specifically grown to be picked while still very small. Pickled in vinegar, they have a tart flavor and crisp texture.

CRÈME FRAÎCHE A soured cultured cream product, originally from France, crème fraîche is similar to sour cream but more subtle and indulgent. French and domestic brands of crème fraîche are available at many well-stocked markets, but you can also make it at home. To make crème fraîche, combine 1 cup (8 fl oz/250 ml) heavy (double) cream and 1 tablespoon buttermilk in a small saucepan over medium-low heat. Heat just to lukewarm (not above 85°F/29°C), and do not allow to simmer. Remove from the heat, partially cover, and allow to thicken at warm room temperature, which can take from 8 to 48 hours. The longer it sits, the thicker and tangier it will become. Refrigerate for 3–4 hours to chill before using. It will keep for 7–10 days.

DIJON MUSTARD A sharply flavored prepared mustard from the Dijon area in France, Dijon mustard is made primarily from ground brown mustard seeds, white wine and/or white vinegar, and seasonings.

EGG, RAW In some recipes, eggs are used raw or only partially cooked. These eggs run a risk of being infected with salmonella or other bacteria, which can lead to food poisoning. This risk is of most concern to small children, older people, pregnant women, and anyone with a compromised immune system. If you have health and safety concerns, do not consume an undercooked egg, or seek out a pasteurized egg product to replace it. Eggs can also be made safe by heating them to a temperature of 140°F (60°C) for 3½ minutes. Note that coddled, poached, and soft-boiled eggs do not reach this temperature.

GRUYÈRE One of the classic cheeses in a cheese fondue, Gruyère is made in Switzerland from cow's milk. It is pale yellow and has a nutty yet mild flavor and firm texture.

HARICOTS VERTS Literally translated from the French, haricots verts are green beans. Also called filet beans, haricots verts are a small, slender variety with a delicate flavor and tender texture.

KOSHER SALT These pure coarse rock salt granules are a bit larger than poppy seeds and contain no additives. Kosher salt has a clean taste and is not as strong as regular table salt. If using regular table salt, use only half the amount called for in the recipes in this book.

MASHER, HANDHELD Considered by many cooks to be the preferred tool to use for mashing potatoes, a handheld masher yields mashed potatoes with a coarse texture. It will not overwork the potatoes, which can result in a dense, gluey consistency. Look for a masher with a sturdy handle and a mashing grid with some flat portions to help purée the potato lumps more efficiently.

MUSHROOMS
Cremini: These darker, fuller-flavored versions of the common cultivated white mushroom are usually 1–2 inches (2.5–5 cm) in diameter with a smooth round cap. They are also known as Italian or brown mushrooms.

Portobello: Mature cremini, portobello mushrooms are 3–5 inches (7.5–13 cm) in diameter and can sometimes be even larger. They have flat caps and exposed brownish black gills. Their flavor is rich, earthy, and even meaty. A smaller variety, often labeled baby portobello, is about 2½ inches (6 cm) in diameter. Discard the stems or reserve for making stock and scoop out the gills to avoid giving your dish a dark cast.

Shiitake: These brown, tender mushrooms native to Japan are now grown in the United States and measure 2–5 inches (5–13 cm) in diameter. They have a rich and somewhat smoky taste. The woody stems are always trimmed off. Other names for the shiitake are golden oak, forest, and Chinese black.

MUSTARD POWDER Mustard seeds come in three colors: white (also called yellow), brown, and black. The white seeds are the mildest, followed in pungency by brown and black. English mustard powder is the preferred form of mustard powder and is a classic blend of ground white and brown seeds with some added wheat flour.

NUTMEG See page 13.

ONIONS
Green: Also known as scallions or spring onions, green onions are slender and long, with a single small white bulb topped with several hollow green stalks. Their bright, mild flavor can be enjoyed raw as well as cooked.

Red: Also called Bermuda onions or Italian onions, red onions are actually scarlet in color. They are sweeter than yellow onions, are popular sliced raw in salads and sandwiches, and are mild when cooked.

Shallot: See page 22.

White: More pungent than the red onion, but milder and less sweet than the yellow, the white onion is the favorite of the Mexican cook. Large, slightly flattened, mild white onions are sometimes called white Spanish onions.

Yellow: The yellow globe onion is the common, all-purpose onion sold in supermarkets. It can be globular, flattened, or slightly elongated and has parchmentlike golden brown skin. It becomes rich and sweet when cooked, making it ideal for caramelizing.

PARSLEY Two types of parsley are commonly available: curly-leaf parsley and flat-leaf, or Italian, parsley. The latter has a more pronounced bright, fresh flavor and is preferred for recipes in this cookbook.

PARSNIP See page 33.

POTATOES, TYPES See pages 105–6.

POTATO RICER A ricer is composed of a small pot with a perforated bottom and a plunger attached to the rim. The plunger forces the potatoes or other softly cooked root vegetables through the holes. The result is soft rice-size particles that, when stirred, produce a smooth texture.

ROSEMARY A Mediterranean herb, rosemary looks like pine needles on a woody stick. This herb has an assertive flavor that pairs well with lamb, many vegetables, and seafood, but it should be used in moderation. Dried rosemary is very bland compared to fresh, but if used, the hard dry needles should be finely crumbled.

SAFFRON Some authorities claim it takes nearly 14,000 hand-harvested stigmas from about 4,300 small purple crocus flowers to yield 1 oz (30 g) of saffron, making this one of the world's most expensive spices. To make sure you have a high-quality product, buy and use only thread saffron (whole stigmas), not the powdered variety, which can easily be adulterated with other ingredients. Saffron has a pungent, earthy, and slightly bitter flavor. Although orange-red in color, the stigmas lend a lovely yellow color to many dishes.

SEEDS

Caraway: These dark brown seeds come from an herb in the parsley family, are about ¼ inch (6 mm) long, and carry an aroma immediately associated with rye bread. Caraway seeds are used extensively in German, Hungarian, and Austrian cooking.

Fennel: These muted green, ridged seeds have a delicate anise flavor. They are commonly used to season Italian sausages as well as other sweet and savory dishes and liqueurs.

SKIMMER With a long handle and a large flat strainer or shallow bowl of wire mesh, a skimmer is designed to remove the scum or foam from the top of simmering stocks. It is also perfect for scooping a great number of gnocchi, French fries, or other small pieces of food from boiling water or hot oil.

SOUR CREAM Sour cream is cream that has been deliberately soured. By adding a bacterial culture to cream, producers can control the souring process as the lactose in the cream converts to lactic acid. Commercial sour cream, consisting of 18 to 20 percent butterfat, has a thick, creamy texture that makes it popular for baking, in dressings, and for topping finished dishes. It is especially good with potatoes.

STEAMER BASKET See page 108.

THYME Tiny green leaves on thin stems, this herb is a mild, all-purpose seasoning. Its floral, earthy flavor complements meats, fish, vegetables, and salads. If a large amount is needed, gently pull the leaves backward off the stem. When the thyme stems are very soft, just chop them with the leaves.

TOASTING NUTS AND SEEDS To toast pine nuts and other types of nuts and seeds without turning on the oven, place a small amount in a dry frying pan on the stove top. Toast over medium-low heat, stirring frequently, until fragrant and beginning to color. Depending on the type of nut or seed and the size of the pieces, this may take 2–8 minutes. Keep a close eye on them, for they burn quickly. Immediately transfer to a plate or paper towel to cool. Nuts and seeds continue to toast while cooling, so remove them from the heat when they are just a shade lighter than desired. They will become darker and crisper as they cool. Store toasted nuts and seeds in an airtight container for 3 days at room temperature or refrigerate for up to 10 days.

TOMATOES, SEEDING See page 102.

INDEX

SIMON & SCHUSTER SOURCE
A Division of Simon & Schuster, Inc.
Rockefeller Center
1230 Avenue of the Americas
New York, NY 10020

WILLIAMS-SONOMA
Founder and Vice-Chairman: Chuck Williams
Book Buyer: Cecilia Prentice

WELDON OWEN INC.
Chief Executive Officer: John Owen
President: Terry Newell
Chief Operating Officer: Larry Partington
Vice President, International Sales: Stuart Laurence
Creative Director: Gaye Allen
Series Editor: Sarah Putman Clegg
Project Editor: Heather Belt
Art Director: Catherine Jacobes
Designer: Kyrie Forbes
Production Manager: Chris Hemesath
Shipping and Production Coordinator: Libby Temple
Photograph Editor: Lisa Lee

Weldon Owen wishes to thank the following
people for their generous assistance and
support in producing this book: Copy Editor
Carolyn Miller; Consulting Editor Sharon Silva;
Designer Douglas Chalk; Food Stylists Kim Konecny
and Erin Quon; Photographer's Assistant Faiza Ali;
Proofreaders Desne Ahlers, Carrie Bradley, and
Linda Bouchard; and Indexer Ken DellaPenta.

Williams-Sonoma Collection *Potato* was
conceived and produced by Weldon Owen Inc.,
814 Montgomery Street, San Francisco,
California 94133, in collaboration with
Williams-Sonoma, 3250 Van Ness Avenue,
San Francisco, California 94109.

A Weldon Owen Production
Copyright © 2002 by Weldon Owen Inc. and
Williams-Sonoma Inc.

For information about special discounts for bulk
purchases, please contact Simon & Schuster
Special Sales: 1-800-456-6798 or
business@simonandschuster.com

Set in Trajan, Utopia, and Vectora.

Color separations by Bright Arts Graphics
Singapore (Pte.) Ltd.
Printed and bound in Singapore by Tien Wah Press
(Pte.) Ltd.

First printed in 2002.

10 9 8 7 6 5 4 3 2 1

Library of Congress Cataloging-in-Publication Data

Morrow, Selma Brown.
   Potato / recipes and text, Selma Brown Morrow ;
general editor, Chuck Williams ; photographs,
Maren Caruso.
      p. cm. — (Williams-Sonoma collection)
   Includes index.
   1. Cookery (Potatoes) I. Williams, Chuck.
II. Title. III. Williams-Sonoma collection
(New York, N.Y.)

TX803.P8 M67 2002
641.6'521—dc21
                                    2002023023
ISBN 0-7432-2682-8

A NOTE ON WEIGHTS AND MEASURES

All recipes include customary U.S. and metric measurements. Metric conversions are based on
a standard developed for these books and have been rounded off. Actual weights may vary.